Your Modern Guide for Epic American Adventures

*Empowering you to create life changing roadtrips
through simplifying the planning process
and offering crucial insight.*

Guiding you to get the most out of each experience.

Jonathan Simos

HowToRoadTripAmerica.com

Copyright © 2019 by Jonathan Simos

All rights reserved.

No part of this book may be reproduced, scanned, or distributed in any printed or electronic form without permission.

Printed in the United States of America

ISBN: 978-1-939237-68-2

Published by Suncoast Digital Press, Inc.

Sarasota, Florida, USA

Dedication

To Lauren Assang and Bella

Because love is something eternal, the aspect may change but not the essence. (I know you aren't fond of that quote, but it is true.)

I am grateful for our time together and every part of our journey that we shared, allowing us both much growth and many life changing experiences. Thank you for bringing me on a three-year adventure with you...living in different cities allowed us to routinely take epic roadtrips across the nation. These adventures truly opened up my eyes and allowed me to feel credible enough to write this book to help others experience the same wonders.

*I appreciate all of the beautiful pictures you took
that I am now able to share with others,
to inspire them to pursue similar experiences across the nation.*

*Thank you for being supportive despite the ups and downs
of my entrepreneurial journey. I will forever be grateful
for everything we shared and experienced.*

I hope you enjoy this book dedicated to you.

Contents

— PART 1 —

Chapter 1
Introduction...1

Background...5

Chapter 2
The Ever-Changing Landscape...11

Chapter 3
Clear Your Mind, Free Your Soul, And Gain New Perspectives...17

Chapter 4
Roadtrippin' Through History...23

Chapter 5
Commandments of Roadtrippin'...31

Chapter 6
It's All About The Journey...43

— PART 2 —

Chapter 7
Choose Your Own Adventure...85

Chapter 8
Charts and Maps...95

Chapter 9
Creating The Foundation...103

Chapter 10
Building an Epic Trip...109

Chapter 11
Preparing...115

Chapter 12
The Nitty Gritty...123

Chapter 13
A Taste of Freedom...141

— PART 3 —

Chapter 14
Roughing It!...149

Chapter 15
The Art of Conversation...157

Chapter 16
The Art of Being...163

Chapter 17
On The Trip Home...173

Chapter 18
Follow Your Heart...177

Chapter 19
Fun Facts...183

Chapter 20
Your Upcoming Adventures...189

Acknowledgments...192

About the Author...195

"Life is a magical journey, so travel endlessly to unfold its profound and heart touching beauty."

—Debasish Mridha

Driving to Mount Tallac, passing Emerald Bay
South Lake Tahoe, California

PART 1

"Travel makes one modest. You see what a tiny place you occupy in the world."

—*Gustav Flaubert*

Chapter 1

INTRODUCTION

The American roadtrip is truly classic: a signature adventure with friends, family, or alone, it was once deemed impossible until only the last century. With the vast benefits that a roadtrip offers, along with advancements in technology and improvements in roads and attractions, we are living in the perfect age to take advantage of this luxury.

The truth is, wherever you live in America you are within range of taking a once-in-a-lifetime roadtrip and experiencing the vast benefits of the open road and all that it entails. You can even take an epic roadtrip within a short amount of time, from a day or weekend trip to an extensive one, as long as you follow key guidelines.

America is such a beautiful country that allows countless life changing experiences from breathtaking views, majestic redwood forests and other drastically changing terrain to the varying subcultures associated within each region. There are vast opportunities to learn about the food, art, local communities, historical places, activities, and so much more. The list is truly endless!

Roadtrips are on the rise again as many travelers are recognizing the goldmine that they have in their own backyards; the vast benefits and local adventures simply awaiting them around the corner. Would be travelers understand that a roadtrip is a trip like no other, allowing the freedom of maximum spontaneity—to stop wherever, whenever—among other advantages that flying to a destination simply cannot provide. It's a part of human nature—focusing on the journey, rather than just the destination— teaching us to live in the moment.

On the other hand, many people are still intimidated by the thought of a roadtrip and choose instead to book a flight across the country or even overseas to their destination without even considering driving or other methods by which to travel. This typically stems from a misconception that a roadtrip requires extensive planning and weeks off, which only contributes to the overwhelm they may be feeling along with not knowing where to start.

These fears may also stem from, "That one time...," a traumatic childhood experience of feeling trapped in the backseat for countless hours in a roadtrip done wrong. I'm here to tell you, based on experience from both sides, these are irrational fears and a roadtrip should never be this way if done properly.

- 51% of vacationers admit they are stressed, according to a study by Wyndham Vacation Rentals, with the top stressors being:

- 61% are concerned with spending too much money

- 49% are clueless about the packing process

- 48% are stressed about keeping everyone happy and entertained

- 46% are worried about finding accommodations

- 98% prioritize clean bathrooms, and worry about finding them

That is exactly the reason I wrote this book, to break down these fears and misconceptions and assure you that a roadtrip never has to be negative, as there is truly a right way and a wrong way to take one. If you attempt one the wrong way, you will miss out on the best experiences and make it a trip rather than a journey. When done correctly, however, each and every one can be life changing and therapeutic, easing stress, freeing your soul, and even strengthening relationships. Roadtrips should be refreshing rather than exhausting, and they should always be exhilarating rather than boring.

Chapter 1: Introduction

Roadtrips are symbolic of life, teaching us to live in the present and enjoy every moment along the journey rather than only focusing on the destination. Each adventure will be full of different experiences that ultimately have the power to change your perspective and be a catalyst for immense growth. I wrote this book because many individuals, couples, and families miss out on these special moments and growth together.

This book will break down misconceptions by offering awareness of the benefits that these trips entail, along with providing simple and clear directions to allow you to create your dream adventure in just a series of steps, simplifying the planning process while offering crucial insight to follow as well.

Use this book to plan your first or next roadtrip and be sure to bring it along with you on your adventures.

BACKGROUND

Growing up my family would take an epic roadtrip across America nearly every year. Sometimes it was done in a very small vehicle. Pillows were wedged between my brother and I while random items were stacked so high in the back window that you could not see out. We often would drive on a mission to get to our destination which meant longer drive times and fewer breaks. Driving through countless cities was amazing, though definitely not always sunshine and smiles! We would experience every emotion imaginable as my brother and I would argue endlessly over backseat territory, among other things. However, with that being said, we also had amazing times and once-in-a-lifetime experiences as a family. For that I am grateful, along with beginning to learn different aspects of roadtrips, and how to improve each one.

As a young adult in my late teens and early twenties with an insatiable desire to explore, I was compelled to constantly travel within my means and did so on smaller roadtrips. These trips usually consisted of campus hopping across Florida to visit friends that I had at various colleges. From each of these experiences I learned a lot about how to take a solo trip in the best and most efficient manner.

In my mid to late-twenties, I began to date a wonderful young lady who worked as a traveling nurse. We both had the travel bug so after dating a little while we took off from Sarasota, Florida, in an impulsive decision to travel and move across the country together to a new city that neither of us had ever been to—Los Angeles! Though it could have ended differently, it turned out to be one of the best experiences of our lives and we continued to take trips every chance we got.

Throughout every part of California, back to Florida, across America a handful of times and even exploring the Southeast and Northeast, we covered nearly every corner of this nation along with her 65-pound boxer named Bella, who would hibernate in the backseat with her big, floppy ears.

With each trip we became more efficient, more resourceful and more comfortable, and we learned how to plan an ultimate trip based off of the general theme and experiences we wanted. After L.A., we lived in Austin, Texas, before finding our way back to San Diego, California, for nine more months before returning to Florida. Within that time frame we did more trips than one can imagine…and practice makes perfect!

We perfected how to plan, what to bring, what not to bring, how to pack the vehicle (proper placement makes essentials easy to get to while driving), how to leverage technology, and the list goes on!

As for the trips, they were amazing. Our travels took us from deserts to beautiful mountains, along breathtaking routes where deer would cross the road in front of us, to hidden detours that took us past small fruit stands that offered an assortment of local produce. We had excursions through redwood forests, under waterfalls, and autumn adventures in search of breathtaking foliage. A few trips even took us down unbeaten paths where we may have heard Bigfoot (I swear).

We took both well-planned trips and spontaneous trips that did not have a destination or a singular purpose—other than perhaps simply chasing the first snowstorm of the winter season…all in a silver 2013 Nissan Sentra that my girlfriend had named Lucy.

Lucy looked like she had been through hell and back, and she truly had. Her rear bumper was attached with duct tape. Neither her right nor left side mirror was attached—one fell off as the result of a driving mishap while the other fell victim to late night scandal. How we survived off-roading in Lucy while taking her down snow laden roads and through shallow streams, I'm not quite sure. In conclusion, we experienced much and I'm here to tell you how to plan the trip of your life and learn to appreciate the open road along with all of the wonders around you.

Seeing both sides, how amazing these trips could be when done right and how much is taken away from them when they are not done right, there's definitely a right and a wrong way to do things just like anything else as I previously mentioned. I was inspired to write this book because a roadtrip is one of the most influential trips that one can take and, being in America, there are countless opportunities.

I've simplified the planning process by reducing it to a foundation of **eight steps** before proceeding. You will also learn **"The 26 Commandments of Roadtripping"** and how to best take advantage of current technology, using a chart and map for perspective, gain insight on various mobile apps, and understand the steps and details of proper planning. For your convenience, this book also simplifies the packing process and offers checklists on what to bring. And I know at some point you will appreciate plenty of other resources in Chapter 6 from the list of interactive questions and games during downtime, to music lists and much more.

Each of the three sections will include one brief personal story, many resources, and additional insight. The initial reading of this book will change your perspective of and help you gain a new appreciation for roadtrips, but my hope is that it will continue to be a resource for you. You will be able to refer back and utilize all the resources in the back of the book as a quick reference guide for each consecutive trip.

You will understand the vast psychological benefits of a roadtrip previously mentioned and you'll also learn to use the simplified planning process to seamlessly create your dream trip each and every time, ultimately empowering you with the confidence and knowledge to take your epic roadtrip!

Chapter 1: Background

YOUR MODERN GUIDE FOR ROADTRIPPIN'

Hiking Mount Tallac, finding the first snow of the season in South Lake Tahoe, California

"The real voyage of discovery consists not in seeking new landscapes, but in having new eyes."

– Marcel Proust

Chapter 2

THE EVER-CHANGING LANDSCAPE

My first life-changing roadtrip experience

Going, going, back, back to Cali…

I was 12 years old, and I was just coming home from playing with neighborhood friends in the humid Florida, pre-summer heat. I found my mother at the kitchen table, working on plans for our biennial roadtrip. Being a creative type, she loved designing these intricate travel plans with all that they entailed.

Mom would construct a vast layout of dots and lines on a map that almost made her seem like a detective trying to solve a crime. Upon seeing this, I was overcome with mixed emotions as I had a love/hate relationship with these long trips. The downside was feeling stuck in the backseat since my family would rarely stop and was always destination driven; yet, on the good side I would also remember amazing experiences in my first shorter trip that included seeing bears and deer, finding waterfalls on hikes in NC, and much more.

We took off that May on a four-week expedition that would take us from our hometown of Sarasota, Florida, up through the southern states of Georgia, the Carolinas, and eventually up to visit family in New York City, New York. The next destination was to see more relatives, this time on my mother's side, down in Missouri.

Once leaving the corn fields of the Midwest, we made our way west through Colorado and then through northern California. Eventually we made it through the southern part of the United States. This trip was a grand one and pretty much covered every region of the Contiguous US.

My father loved driving and could somehow summon an inner race car driver from within, covering countless miles across often endless terrains. I oftentimes believed he liked to feel as if he was racing as he drove quickly across the winding mountain roads and vast landscapes, never wanting to stop! Fortunately he is a great driver and I always felt comfortable with him in the driver's seat, though I had to learn how to survive these long trips through preparation, bringing the softest pillow I could find and as many books and miscellaneous items that I could fit with me in my small space.

This reflection was more valuable to my 12-year-old self than I could have ever anticipated. It allowed me to begin a journey of self-discovery along with learning how to process past experiences for growth. Thinking about the big picture as a whole and how tiny we were as we slowly moved along our route somewhere in America was truly both humbling and eye opening.

As the trip continued the terrain began to reshape, with larger, taller trees, and hilly inclines turning into mountains. In slow motion, America revealed her vast beauty. It was an experience in itself to watch the landscape transform from flat Florida swamps to the forested mountains of North Carolina, and then contract into overpasses heavy with traffic, city lights, and the skyscraping skyline as we headed for New York City. At every pit stop one could not help but notice how different the people were. They talked differently and dressed differently. The overall feel was entirely different from one gas station to the next.

Arriving in New York City I was awestruck. I had never seen so many people in one place! Every block was covered with people all going somewhere, like ants in an anthill. It was organized chaos! It was an intriguing and beautiful scene to watch as the never-ending flow of people just streamed by, each person with his or her own destination and purpose. We stayed a couple of days with family whom I had never met before, yet wished I had met years prior. I played with cousins my age who were a lot of fun and were in a very nice, friendly, neighborhood community. We also drove past different areas that ranged from run-down apartments to expensive homes on Long Island. All of these experiences put everything into perspective as you could see the vast differences in lifestyles—some drastic from one block to the next.

Leaving the city behind, we headed west and soon found immense changes in the terrain. We found ourselves in the rolling hills of the Midwest, and it was fascinating how quickly the landscape could change, sometimes dramatically, within only an hour! After spending a couple of days passing through the open plains, I awoke from a nap to view a vast desert with yellowish sand dunes stretched across the horizon as far as the eye could see!

I remember falling asleep to the lulling of the road and waking up to my mother screaming "Look! Deer!!" The majestic sand dunes were gone and we were now in a mountainous environment where a little family of deer walked across the road in front of us. It was then I noticed it was cold!

We continued to climb in elevation until we reached a point where it seemed as if we drove into Narnia. Yes, there was snow—so much snow! It was a different world and we were in a blizzard somewhere in the mountains! I yelled, "STOP!" at the top of my lungs as I shifted to try to take off my seat belt and position myself for a fast exit. My dad pulled over and I launched out of the car into the snow, wearing just shorts and a t-shirt. It was a truly amazing experience and it was freezing! I played in the snow as long as I could and once I could no longer feel my hands I jumped back in and we continued on.

We continued on towards California; however, at this point, I was already a different person. This trip was a humbling experience that got me out of my simple-minded routine as a child and allowed me to see how big the world truly is. There is something very powerful about crossing the terrain slowly in a vehicle and being able to watch it change before your eyes, as opposed to flying and missing the journey.

This vacation allowed me to begin my journey of self-discovery by providing time where I couldn't look externally for stimulation but was forced to look within and ask introspective questions, learning more about who I was. The trip also humbled me and showed me how much is going on in the world and it made me appreciate the life that I had, while strengthening relationships with loved ones as we were forced to work and experience everything together. In conclusion, aside from the learning experiences, it gave me insight and greater understanding, an open mind, and pushed me to look within and learn how to reflect and process information.

Chapter 2: The ever-changing landscape

"Life begins at the end of your comfort zone.

—Neale Donald Walsch

Chapter 3

CLEAR YOUR MIND, FREE YOUR SOUL, AND GAIN NEW PERSPECTIVES

Appreciating the vast benefits of the open road

From an overlook in Yosemite National Park

The classic roadtrip is much more than just a vacation. It is symbolic of life, reminding us that it's about the moments and experiences along the journey rather than the destination. It's the epitome of being free and living in the present, with the open road in front of you. There are no obligations, expectations, or stress when it is done right.

IT'S IN OUR NATURE

The desire to roam freely and explore new lands is truly in our nature as humans, though the degree of wanderlust seems to vary throughout society. There are those that enjoy occasional trips but prefer to stay close to home, while others are the free spirits who can't sit still and have a burning desire to travel far and wide.

"From a very primal point of view, humans are nomadic by nature," said psychologist Christine Bagley-Jones, director of the Counselling and Wellbeing Centre in Brisbane.

Extreme wanderlust may be explained by epigenetics, or "the study of changes in organisms caused by modification of gene expression rather than alteration of the genetic code itself." (Webster online dictionary.) It has even recently been associated with a gene called DRD4-7R, which affects dopamine levels in the brain. It has been nicknamed the "wanderlust gene," or "adventure gene," because of its correlation with increased levels of restlessness and desire to explore. According to research, this gene is prevalent in about 20% of the population. Any given family could have one member who is obsessed with travel, who simply cannot understand why everyone else lacks the same thirst for adventure.

National Geographic supported these findings in a study done by David Dobbs. He discovered that this gene is typically found in those who migrated further over the course of thousands of years, rather than populations which stayed rooted. Whether you have this gene or not, traveling is beneficial for everyone, and roadtrips have the best potential for unique and fulfilling experiences.

SELF-GROWTH

Within all the characteristics of roadtrips they can teach you mindfulness, independence, and boost confidence among many other lessons. Roadtrips force you to be open minded, be an observer of life, let go and simply live. Studies have shown that roadtrips actually boost your creativity by immersing you in different environments and cultures while allowing you to embrace different ways of living than your own. They immediately push you out of your comfort zone, allowing growth and changing your personality to be much more adaptable. Each trip can provide lessons in patience when dealing with traffic jams or delays, flat tires or other circumstances beyond your control, while challenging you to be open to adapting to new opportunities.

Later in this book, in Chapter 16 titled: "The Art of Being," I will list exercises to enhance reflection and self-growth.

HEALTH

Stress relief is provided by the open road because you are out of your old routine and environment, resetting both your body and mind. You are free of obligation and expectation and forced to simply live in the moment. Studies have shown that people tend to be happier when anticipating a travel experience as opposed to purchasing a new item or product. This reinforces the value of these experiences! Roadtrips have much more value than a simple flight to a destination because they have the potential to offer spontaneity and, ultimately, more interesting experiences.

There is growing evidence that "disconnecting" has health benefits, as well. If you are on a roadtrip there is less compulsion to be on your phone, checking emails or social media constantly. You are free to listen to music or an audio book, have deep conversations and get to know one another on a new level, or just tune out, and enjoy the view.

"Getting away from it all" can work wonders for stress reduction. According to *Forbes Magazine*, taking vacations lowers the risk of death by 21% in men and mortality from cardiovascular disease by 32%. Women that travel frequently are less tense and happier overall. Despite these benefits, 52% of Americans had remaining days left last year from their employer, failing to take advantage of time off to relax and perhaps travel with the intention of simply appreciating new surroundings.

Even though many believe that sitting for long periods may cause health issues, these trips don't have to take a negative toll as long as you follow the roadtrip commandments listed later in this book and stop every two hours to briefly stretch your legs and enhance your circulation with a couple exercises, while also choosing healthy snacks and remaining active throughout each trip.

CONNECT ON A DIFFERENT LEVEL WITHIN RELATIONSHIPS

Roadtrips strengthen existing relationships and help to form new ones by sharing special moments with friends and loved ones on the road while getting to know them better. They also teach you to appreciate all types of people and their differences, providing the opportunity to connect with others without any expectations and value interactions. You can simply enjoy your present conversation with a stranger at a gas station, the connection of the moment as you ask for local insight or simply say hello. Whether this is at a local coffee shop or gas station, asking somebody directions can turn into a rich conversation where you gain insights into the area's history, the people, where to go locally, and what is a must-see.

You learn to appreciate the various dynamics of relationships in the world, and also people in general. Sometimes you will want to form longer-term relationships by taking advantage of social media and keeping in touch with those where more than a causal connection was made. You may gain some quality, long-term friends across the nation! If you're taking a solo trip, you could meet many others and there is even more room for self-growth.

When it comes to traveling with a significant other, friends, or family, any roadtrip will drastically impact your relationship with that person or those loved ones. There is no better way to get to know and understand another person on a much deeper level than to spend countless hours with them on a journey. You will be challenged with working together on tasks while interacting in a variety of situations. These trips provide opportunities to enjoy once-in-a-lifetime experiences together while also allowing time to ask quality questions to better understand one another. Later in the book in Chapter 6, you will find resources for games and questions to ask each other to not only take advantage of downtime, but also to deepen the relationships with your fellow trippers.

HAPPINESS AND FULFILLMENT

Happiness and fulfillment basically comes down to having four essentials: self-improvement, relationships, new experiences, and giving back. A roadtrip has the potential to have all four of these components that contribute to happiness and fulfillment in your life. Part of self-improvement is personal growth, which is always an outcome of a roadtrip while also putting yourself to the test and allowing self-discovery, giving you more clarity about your life's desires, direction, and purpose.

Aside from the benefits, the ultimate purpose of a roadtrip is to experience everything the environment has to offer. It's all about immersing yourself and learning about the history of the regions you are passing through, experiencing the culture, trying the foods, checking out the parks and historic sites and interacting with locals. All of these things make a roadtrip unique and allow you to enjoy each aspect of the journey.

OFFERS PERSPECTIVE AND HEALING

In a book named by *Time* magazine as one of 100 best-selling English language novels, *On the Road,* by Jack Kerouac, the reader is drawn in and reminded of the special ability that roadtrips have to awaken something within each of us. Roadtrips have a beginning and yet uncertain end. Because of this, they can be exhilarating and remind us that barriers often only exist in our minds as we transcend across different landscapes.

"Sal, we gotta go and never stop going till we get there."

"Where we going, man?"

"I don't know but we gotta go."

—Jack Kerouac, *On the Road*

Roadtrips provide time to heal in many ways. You may be dealing with the loss of a loved one or some other traumatic event

*"A good traveler
has no fixed plans,
and is not intent on arriving."*

– Lao Tzu

Chapter 4

ROADTRIPPIN' THROUGH HISTORY

A brief history and timeline

*Target practice or shootout?
Bullet-ridden classic cars on the way to Meteor Crater in Arizona*

Roadtripping Preceded Car Travel

In America in the 1800's and early 1900's, travel outside of established towns and cities was very rough and adventurous. There were few passable trails or roads, and the distance one could cover in a day was very limited, by today's standards. Yet early American history is largely defined by our ancestors' compulsion to roadtrip.

In the mid-19th century, coach travel that changed horses several times a day carried mail and passengers long distances. By stagecoach, the

2800-mile distance from Saint Louis to San Francisco on the southern Butterfield Overland Route could be completed in 23 to 25 days (a little over 100 miles a day).

Stations at which a coach could get a fresh driver and horses were established about one day's ride apart. Even earlier in history, the Spanish constructed a string of missions purposely to be one day's ride apart by horse. There were over 20, including Los Angeles and San Francisco. The longest distance between any two is 59 miles (from La Purisima Mission to Mission San Luis Obispo de Tolosa).

With the advent of travel via passenger train (powered by steam), much longer distances could be covered in a day, as long as you wanted to go to one of the places trains happened to go.

THE HORSELESS CARRIAGE COMES ON THE SCENE

Most Americans could not afford early automobiles and there were limited fueling stations and amenities outside city limits. The introduction of Henry Ford's Model T began to revolutionize the industry. Automobiles became more accessible as wages increased, but the rocky, muddy and pothole-covered roads still required an adventurous soul. Not only were cars expensive, but there weren't any roads on which to drive them.

Despite the initial negative perceptions, between 1900 and 1915, the number of cars in America jumped from just 8,000 to more than 2 million. The Ford Motor Company produced 14 million Model T's between 1913 and 1927.

Yet, the first patent for a motorized vehicle and the first recorded roadtrip by car have their place in Germany's history, not America's. The pioneers of automobile manufacturing were Gottlieb Daimler (1834-1900) and Karl Benz (1844-1929). The first distance trip in an automobile was done by the wife of Karl Benz, Bertha Benz, in Germany in 1888. She did a 66-mile trip in an experimental Benz motor car that had a maximum speed of 10 mph. In her great feat, she drew worldwide attention and got the company its first sales.

The first roadtrip in North America was significantly longer, more expensive, and full of hardships and tremendous challenges. Reading about this journey across our country is fascinating (especially compared to Bertha Benz' 66-mile excursion). Below is an excerpt from an article on the History Channel's web site (https://www.history.com/news/):

"In the early afternoon of May 23, 1903, Horatio Nelson Jackson and Sewall Crocker slid into the front seat of a gleaming, cherry-red Winton touring car and chugged down San Francisco's Market Street amid a sea of horse-drawn carriages. The sleeping bags, cooking gear, and supplies packed inside the automobile testified to a long journey ahead, but the roadtrip on which the men were embarking was truly epic—an unprecedented cross-country drive to New York City.

"And it all started with a $50 wager.

"Just four days before, a bar debate about the newfangled horseless carriages ignited inside San Francisco's exclusive University Club. While most of the tipplers dismissed the automobile as a passing novelty too unreliable to survive a trip across America, Jackson disagreed.

"Then…someone bet Jackson $50 that he couldn't make it to New York City by car in less than 90 days. The 31-year-old automobile enthusiast from Burlington, Vermont, who had given up his medical practice after a bout of tuberculosis—heartily accepted.

"Jackson recruited Crocker, a 22-year-old former bicycle racer and a gasoline engine mechanic, to accompany him. Based on Crocker's recommendation, the former physician purchased a used 20-horsepower Winton touring car for the treacherous journey. Jackson named his new wheels the 'Vermont.'"

Can you imagine the determination it would have taken to accomplish such a roadtrip back then? Fewer than 150 miles of roads nationwide were paved. There were no road signs, road numbers, or roadside service and gas stations, and automobiles were extremely prone to breakdowns.

Think about these breakdowns for a moment. Just 15 miles into their journey, they had a flat tire and replaced it with their only spare. Along the way, they had many, many parts fail or break, and if they couldn't find a blacksmith to make the repair, they had to wait for a stage coach or train to deliver the part to them.

Wrong turns and breakdowns, such as a broken clutch and a clogged oil line, slowed their progress. Once, after they found themselves stranded for eight hours in the Oregon desert, a cowboy lassoed the disabled Winton and had his horse give it a tow—an equine version of roadside service.

All of the first American long-distance car travelers must have had a true pioneer spirit. They had to pack all kinds of gear, from cooking supplies to camping accessories, since there were few places to purchase anything in between cities. No 7-11's, no Cracker Barrels, no Ramada Inns.

"Automobiling," said the Brooklyn Eagle newspaper in 1910, was "the last call of the wild."

As these early roadtrippers became more prevalent, fueling stations and supply stores began to pop up in opportune locations to cater to the growing demand. As it became more convenient, road travel grew more popular. Local governments began to use tax dollars to make improvements to roads, signage, and areas of interest for the very first wave of automobile-driving "tourists." However, for each paved road there were still thousands of miles of gravel roads.

Though roadtrips were growing in popularity, the open road wasn't always a safe place. Especially for women and minorities, driving through remote areas was perilous, and even some towns were inhospitable or dangerous. Women were vulnerable to being stopped and robbed, just as passengers on a stage coach or train in earlier times were held up by bandits. African-Americans faced discrimination at most places for lodging, even at campgrounds. They had to plan very carefully to avoid being turned away at certain establishments. This was such a problem that a postal worker named Victor H. Green saw the value in writing a book as a guide for African-Americans who planned on taking a roadtrip. He provided travel tips as well as advice as to which towns should be avoided and which were more welcoming. Published in 1936, this book was titled, *The Negro Motorist Green Book*.

THE FAMILY CAR COMES OF AGE

In the 1920's, owning automobiles and using them for distance travel became normalized among wealthier Americans. After WWII, it became more mainstream, as post-war prosperity gave more middle class families the means to own at least one car. As the materials, manpower, and manufacturing processes that had been building tanks and everything our military required converted over to focusing on automobiles, the design and reliability of cars improved while the assembly lines helped to make them more affordable and available. Cars which could accommodate more passengers and luggage grew in popularity, and were called "station wagons." Station wagon sales (including the 1957 Chevrolet model, aptly named the "Nomad") were highest in the 1950's–1970's.

More and more families began to view a roadtrip vacation as an economical new possibility, and the best way for children to learn about America and its history by visiting different regions, parks, and historic sites. Trips started to take on a new meaning. Coinciding with the increase in family car travel was a boon in the postcard industry. Postcard sales soared as motorists began traveling further afield, collecting and sending images of national landmarks, landscapes, tourist attractions, and roadside imagery. Procuring and writing postcards was one of the first activities for the whole family on the road—just like posting to social media today, it was a way to share (or show off) a little to others missing out on the adventure.

THE DEMAND TO EXPAND

Something happened in the mid-20th century that would impact the future of roadtripping and be the greatest catalyst for its popularity to grow: On June 29, President Dwight Eisenhower signed the Federal-Aid Highway Act of 1956. The bill created a 41,000-mile "National System of Interstate and Defense Highways."

The purpose of this mammoth endeavor was to eliminate unsafe roads, inefficient routes, traffic jams, and all of the other things that got in the way of "speedy, safe transcontinental travel." Also, highway advocates said, "In case of atomic attack on our key cities, the road net would permit quick evacuation of target areas." For all of these reasons, the 1956 law declared that the construction of an elaborate expressway system was "essential to the national interest." It doesn't appear they realized at the time that the interstate system would one day be used for leisure road trips.

According to Richard Ratay, the author of *Don't Make Me Pull Over! An Informal History of the Family Roadtrip,* it took roughly 25 years for the interstate system to resemble what it is today. This network of roads is relatively young. Microwaves have existed longer than America's highway system!

AMERICANS VALUE FREEDOM, INCLUDING EASY MOBILITY

Advancements in America's road quality and quantity, improvements in automobiles, post WWII prosperity, and soldiers returning home from overseas, all contributed to the increase in popularity of roadtrips. As usual, Hollywood reflected America's trend. In 1940's films, or even earlier, a car trip might have a starring role, or be integral to a theme. The road movie keeps its characters "on the move" and often puts the audience in the front seat with a view of the wide open road and dramatically changing scenery, showing that long distances are covered.

Similar to a "Western," road films can be about frontiersmanship and about the codes of discovery (often self-discovery). If you are thinking of watching some classic roadtrip movies to get you in the mood, you've got plenty to choose from! Check out the four Griswold family "Vacation" movies to start. There is no doubt that over the past several decades, Hollywood has boosted the concept, free spirit, and popularity of roadtrips. Roadtrip movies often use the music from the car stereo, which the characters are listening to, as the soundtrack. *Easy Rider* (1969) used a rock soundtrack of songs from Jimi Hendrix, The Byrds, and Steppenwolf. Most roadtrippers today use music to enhance a mood, energize the driver, and/or carry a theme.

The novelty of America's first car-driving vacations did not wear off. Studies show that roadtrips are more popular than ever, with eighty percent of Americans planning to take a 2019 summer roadtrip which, according to AAA (American Automobile Association), is up 10% from last year.

Chapter 4: Roadtrippin' through history

"If you reject the food, ignore the customs, fear the religion and avoid the people, you better stay at home."

- James Michener

Chapter 5

COMMANDMENTS OF ROADTRIPPIN'

26 crucial guidelines to ensure a great roadtrip

Mount Tallac, Lake Tahoe, California

1) It's all about the journey.

Just like in life, a key lesson to remember is that it's about the journey itself rather than just the destination. Focusing on the destination robs you of living in the present. With the end-point on your mind, how can you relax and enjoy the ride? It can cause anxiety that makes you rush through the trip and miss out on so many key experiences. Have the right mindset.

2) Start with a clean and mechanically sound car (and keep it that way).

According to researchers at Princeton University, disorganization and visual clutter— i.e. trash or random stuff rolling around in your vehicle— distracts and causes stress. Dirt and clutter can elevate one's levels of cortisol—the stress hormone—resulting in feelings of fatigue, tiredness, and depression. Conversely, people in clean and organized environments report greater feelings of energy and restfulness. An even more important way to eliminate stress is to have a mechanic check out your car before your trip, with time allowed to make necessary tune-ups and repairs so that you begin the journey with peace of mind about your car's reliability. Have a trashbag handy and make sure to throw away any trash when you stop, keeping your car clean.

3) Get plenty of sleep, especially the night before.

Always get plenty of sleep the night before a roadtrip. There's nothing that will take away from enjoying the open road more than feeling exhausted. If you're tired, you won't have the desire to stop and explore which takes away from the entire premise. It is also very dangerous to be feeling exhausted while at the wheel. Even if you are not the driver, you also want to be well-rested to enjoy the experiences, and to be ready in case you need to take over for the driver.

4) Keep yourself fueled with healthy snacks and water.

Always pack water and healthy snacks, but avoid eating out of boredom. Keeping yourself fueled is one way you can feel your best—nothing amplifies car sickness more than dehydration and unhealthy food. Healthy

Chapter 5: Commandments of roadtrippin'

food helps restore energy and allows you to enjoy the journey. There are specific drinks and foods I highly recommend bringing which are listed in Chapter 12. For example, dark chocolate and coffee are game changers. Dark chocolate (70% cocoa or more) has high antioxidants, flavonoids, and a compound called theobromine. Each of these components works magic in your body. They reduce inflammation and act as a vasodilator which lowers blood flow, increases circulation, and relaxes airways. Dark chocolate and coffee also boost immunity and increase memory and focus. You also feel great when you drink coffee and eat dark chocolate because it releases several neurotransmitters.

5) Always take a break every two hours to at least stretch your legs.

This may sound crazy to some, but pulling over every two hours will keep you fresh and alert so that you can have a safer and more enjoyable journey. Also, it will prevent blood clots which happen occasionally on long flights and cause pulmonary embolisms, which often are fatal. The beauty of driving over flying is you can stop every couple of hours, so do so!

If you have a copilot, switch roles, and no one ends up having to drive more than two straight hours. Make sure you hydrate and drink plenty of water even if you don't feel like it. Often you will be dehydrated and not even know it until you drink water and begin to feel more energized. Stretch your legs and get your circulation going. Keep things interesting by looking around the area, taking a quick hike, or stopping at a historical site or for local food. Make sure when you stop you do the "break ritual" which consists of a couple exercises to get your circulation going and help with mobility. (We'll discuss this further in Commandment #15.)

6) Plan to take your time and enjoy a relaxed trip.

To play it safe, you can give an additional 60-90 minutes of extra drive time to your planned trip timeline for every four hours of driving. For example, if you're driving eight hours to Atlanta and you want to leave at 7am, then in theory you should arrive by 3pm. However, if you add 2.5 hours to your expected trip duration, this extends the arrival time to 5:30pm. Now you can take the suggested breaks, and skip the stress of feeling rushed or like you're "running late." Also, this allows you to take time to stop at various attractions along the way and, if you run into delays due to traffic or road construction, you can still arrive at your destination according to plan.

7) Live in the moment!

Practice mindfulness and living in the moment. If you are not present, you will miss what may be right there in front of you. Making memories is great and it's nice to document them on social media, but do not let technology steal you away from the moment. You can share your experiences with friends and family and reminisce, but there is a time and a place. You can use technology but don't let it use you.

8) Silence is golden.

Let conversations be organic. When the talking ceases, enjoy the silence. There is no need to force it. Nothing will drain you and others more than always feeling the need to fill the silence or entertain one another. If you initiate a conversation and the other person does not seem to fully engage, there is no reason to be persistent. Maybe they are content on their own train of thought and aren't ready to be interrupted . There will be plenty of time later on your journey to talk together.

9) Do not drive more than eight hours or 500 miles in a day (whichever comes first).

Going beyond the eight-hour mark will drain you and only takes away from the whole premise of enjoying the journey. Always try to leave early enough in the morning to allow for driving time, plus stopping time, and arrival before dark. The goal is to leave by 8am so you can arrive at your destination for the evening before 6:30pm when there is still generally sunlight. By doing this you will have the evening to unwind and relax, enjoying the city and still getting a full night's rest before the next day. By following this guideline you will stay well rested and could literally travel countless days without fatigue setting in.

Chapter 5: Commandments of roadtrippin'

10) Avoid driving at night.

Not too many sights can be seen and appreciated in the dark of night. Driving at night means you will miss a lot. You increase your risk of falling asleep, or being in the unfortunate path of other drowsy drivers. It also means you won't be rested and fresh during the next day or days, making that part of the journey less enjoyable. Not knowing the roads and surrounding routes, combined with limited visibility, makes it a dangerous choice. You may be forced to stop at a creepy gas station at night and put yourself in unsafe situations. If you don't already have an overnight place to stay in your plans, there are different mobile apps that make it very easy to find last-minute rooms in the "taking advantage of technology" section in Chapter 6. There is no good reason to ever drive at night, so simply avoid it.

11) Choose your battles, and never fight sleep.

Always stop at the nearest rest stop or take the next exit if you doze off even once! Life is too short to gamble with your life. If you doze off once, it's just a matter of time before you do it again. There are terrible accidents each year because of drivers who fell asleep at the wheel. Coffee can sometimes help, but not always! I recommend bringing some caffeinated beverages with you in your cooler for emergencies; however, you should never get to this point as long as you follow each commandment. Remember to stop every two hours, limit drive time to eight hours in a day, and avoid driving at night.

12) Understand and appreciate the downtime.

There may be periods of time where the cornfields seem like an endless landscape and boredom may try to creep in. This is the only potential downside of roadtrips, but by following my commandments and stopping every two hours and enjoying various viewpoints and attractions, you will stay stimulated and engaged. If there are no real places to stop for diversion, there are many ways to take advantage of the time. In Chapter 6, you will find a list of not-your-everyday questions to take turns asking with your fellow roadtrippers, as well as games and many other ways to appreciate downtime. I'll even provide example time blocks to put it all in perspective.

13) Don't rush.

Drive in the middle lane or slow lane because many extraordinary experiences are born out of spur-of-the-moment choices. You might see something off to the side and decide to take the next exit to check it out. Also, while interstate highways are terrific for travel, often it is nice to take a few back roads instead. Since you are not in a rush, you can explore the countryside you've never seen before. Off the highways, you will almost always find hidden gems. Remember, the point is to savor and enjoy the journey.

14) When you want to turn around, turn around.

Building off of the previous statement, chances are you'll see something that peaks your interest, but not have time to change lanes or pull over safely, so you pass it by. Statistically 95% percent of people keep going! Alright...I made that statistic up but it is probably accurate! Be the 5% and take the extra 5-10 minutes to do a U-turn safely and go check out what initially sparked your interest. Many times in my travels this has led to once-in-a-lifetime experiences.

15) Do the "break ritual" each time you stop.

The break ritual consists of a few exercises that will increase circulation. First, reach your arms over your head and lean (from the waist) to the right and left. Next, rotate left to right 10 times, do 10 repetitions of calf raises, 10 squats, and throw in a hip flexor and calf stretch lastly because sitting for long periods of time can temporarily shorten your hip flexors. The point of stopping every two hours is not only to keep you refreshed or to switch drivers, but it also can prevent blood clots from developing (from sitting too long) that can lead to life threatening pulmonary embolisms! Every year pulmonary embolisms kill thousands of Americans due to blood clots that typically develop in their legs after sitting for long periods of time on a plane. There is a higher risk to older individuals. The risk of a clot increases after a few hours of inactivity so please follow the commandments! The movement gets the circulation going in your legs. Stopping every two hours is sufficient; however, if for some reason you don't stop that often, remain aware of moving your legs every hour or two to keep circulation going after long periods.

Chapter 5: Commandments of roadtrippin'

16) Immerse yourself.

One of the most important aspects of roadtrips is to FULLY immerse yourself in the new environments, experiences, and cultures. Each city and state that you pass through has a unique culture and theme. It is tempting to stick to what you know by listening to your usual music and eating the same foods throughout the entire trip, but you will miss so much. Check out local radio stations and these can reveal the area's unique characteristics. Sample the local food and appreciate the change of scenery by noticing everything about the area and its people that is different from your usual experience. Travel is meant to broaden your horizons and expand your understanding of other people, cultures, and locations, but you have to immerse yourself in the opportunity.

Also, you can create a playlist on Spotify or choose the genre on Pandora that represents the region.

Music is a critical component because it sets the tone and mood of the experience. Imagine that you are on a Christmas getaway. The snowflakes are falling and melting on your cheeks as you make your way to get hot chocolate at a nearby café. What is going to make this experience more nostalgic? Listening to old school hip hop or Christmas music? Music can add to the trip or take away from the experience. Choose to enhance it with music that perfectly captures the energy of the places you are traveling through.

17) Take a new way home when possible.

When planning your trip, determine a different route back for your way home when possible. Doing this allows you to look forward to new upcoming experiences durng the entire road trip.

18) Do research and plan fun stops.

As you research the destination and potential routes before you hit the road, look for attractions you can visit along the way. A long and winding drive up the Blue Ridge Mountain Parkway can include a stop at "Sliding Rock," for example. The key is to always have something to look forward to. If you have a co-pilot, they can search online to see what your next stop may have to offer. Other ideas could come from the local people you speak with at a diner, produce stand, or town square.

19) Use your GPS wisely.

Your GPS is interactive meaning you get out what you put in. Use it to take you to new places that you discover along the way! Simply zoom out your map to see your current whereabouts, local restaurants, and hotspots. If you're on a solo trip, take the opportunity to do a little research on your next break, then check out how far along your route these are with your GPS. This allows excitement and anticipation. Who knows, you may find key spots that were otherwise hidden in your more general research.

20) Switch it up!

A good majority of the trip can be spent enjoying the scenery and change of terrain, and making short stops to take a quick hike, enjoy local food, or see what is offered at a roadside stand—besides picking up some fresh fruit for snacks, you can try local favorites you may never have heard of before, such as mayhaw jelly, boiled peanuts, or zucchini salsa.

Sometimes there will be hours of downtime. A mix of the following always keeps things interesting (choose what suits you based on if you are a solo roadtripper or with one or more companions):

- Google your whereabouts and potential stops

- Set-up a cruising playlist

- Listen to an audiobook or podcast

- Listen to a language teaching program and/or practice with your car buddy

- Tune into your radio and get a sense of the local culture

- Ask quality questions to get to know each other better (See Chapter 6)

- Play a game from the list in Chapter 6

- Use the quiet time to think and reflect

With a good variety, you'll have time to strengthen the relationship with your companion(s), learn new things, and be entertained. There are plenty of options to keep things interesting in each two-hour block.

21) Take pictures!

There is a lot of value in documenting the journey and being able to look back to remember and relive your experiences. You can easily create photo slideshows or albums that will capture your discoveries. Sharing your memories on social media can also bring your experience to your loved ones. Just remember to look up from your screens and enjoy the scenery and the opportunities of the moment. It's best to save posting and going through photos until the end of the trip.

22) Take a big step outside your comfort zone.

If you are someone who loves routines, drinks the same mocha latte every morning, sits in the same seat at Starbucks and gets flustered when someone takes "your" seat, it can be difficult to stray from your normal. There is nothing better to get you out of your routine than a roadtrip. Stepping outside of your comfort zone is always where the most growth, and experiences occur.

Your new territory is where you can gain new insights and expand your perspective. Temporary discomfort is required to experience new sights and sensations. You *will* be uncomfortable when you stop at a tiny one-room restaurant in the middle of Arizona that looks like someone's home, but do it anyway! When you embrace the excitement that goes along with being unsure, this new territory is where wonderful surprises, discoveries, and lasting rewards are found.

23) Walmart is your best friend.

People joke about Walmart, but this business becomes your best friend on a roadtrip. You can find whatever you need at any hour of the night.

Running low on snacks? Need a charger for your phone? Walmart has it. Most are open 24/7 and offer a relatively safe parking lot to sleep in your vehicle if you need an emergency nap. There are numerous locations in every single state, except Hawaii. Be sure to plan ahead, as you can find them in nearly every city except: NYC, Boston, Detroit, San Francisco, and Seattle.

24) Be aware and stay safe.

If you simply know what is going on around you and follow the roadtripping commandments, you won't have to worry about anything. Follow the packing list and you'll have everything that you need. Just pay attention to your environment and follow your intuition. Driving during the day will cut out any sketchy situations that may occur when stopping at gas stations at night in the middle of nowhere. Remember that situations like this are extremely rare.

25) Make new friends.

Locals can be a helpful source of advice and often bring the opportunity for friendship, as long as you are aware and use common sense. If it is obvious that they are on a roadtrip as well, say hello and ask them where they are from and where they are headed. Nothing is better than spontaneous conversations with others.

26) Unplug! Get off your phone.

Give yourself plenty of technology-free time. Nothing will take away from a roadtrip, and defeat the purpose of the venture, more than passengers zoning out on their phones. Only use your phone for a specific reason related to the trip, or to update loved ones on your progress, and then put it away. Choose to talk with your roadtrip partners instead of having long texting sessions with others or being on social media. This is your opportunity to live in the moment, and that includes being present and engaged with where you are and who you are with. Being wrapped up in a cellular device will result in you missing out in a potentially big way. You took this trip for a reason, so get off your phone!

Chapter 5: Commandments of roadtrippin'

"Travel is fatal to narrow-mindedness, prejudice and bigotry."

— Mark Twain

Chapter 6

IT'S ALL ABOUT THE JOURNEY

Getting the most out of each experience, maximizing downtime, and much more

White Sands National Monument in New Mexico

Roadtrips are symbolic of life itself. They are all about enjoying the journey and living in the present moment rather than focusing solely on the destination and having a mindset that emphasizes future events. It is easy to become overly future-oriented and miss out on the gifts of today. A roadtrip is the perfect time to practice enjoying the present, to catch yourself if you are obsessing about when and where you'll arrive instead of creating memories along the way.

If your habit in life is to put things off until you accomplish something else, you will always have some level of anxiety and stress because you "aren't *there* yet." If you always strive to get to your end goal as soon as possible, it takes the happiness and fulfillment out of life because you fail to live in the present. It's great to have a vision and a future goal, but life happens now, not after you reach your goal. The present is our only reality and we must spend our time here in order to enjoy life.

> **"We cannot put off living until we are ready. The most salient characteristic of life is its urgency, 'here and now' without any possible postponement. Life is fired at us point-blank."**
>
> *—Jose Ortega Y Gasset*

Remember life is but a moment and this is it. Your moment is now! It is time to live, love, and experience everything along this journey we call life. Roadtrips help to reinforce this mindset. They allow you to discover much about yourself as you explore various new environments and learn to appreciate the natural beauty and unique qualities of everything around you.

I have learned that the little things in life make all the difference. Roadtrips epitomize that truth. The following practices will give you the tools you need to enjoy the moment and take it all in along your journey:

MAXIMIZE EACH EXPERIENCE

As I keep reiterating, truly getting the most out of every experience simply begins with living in the moment. Step outside of your comfort zone, immerse yourself in your surrounding environment, and be mindful of everything around you.

Memories are great, and it's nice to document your travels on social media for reminiscing purposes and to share your experiences with friends and family; however, there is a time and a place, so keep in mind not to get wrapped up in your phone or computer. This is a time to disconnect and immerse yourself in new environments and new ways of thinking.

When it comes to taking pictures, keep in mind that enjoying the moment is your first and foremost priority. Secondly, after you have taken it all in, then you can think to take a quick picture or two, but don't dwell on it trying to get the perfect picture! It's not a photoshoot! It's about enjoying these moments naturally and sharing them with who you are currently with.

Always be on the lookout for attractions, historic places off a nearby exit, parks, local fruit stands or interesting places! Have someone research the general area and upcoming cities for key places to always have something to look forward to, prior to arrival. Don't be afraid to take an exit and get off your route a few miles to check something out. Remember, that's what it's all about! As long as you follow the commandments you will have plenty of time to get off the interstate and take a hike for 20 or 30 minutes, grab lunch somewhere or even check out a historic site before jumping back in route.

MAXIMIZING THE DOWNTIME

When you are stopping every two hours, stretching your legs and potentially switching drivers, you will only ever have two hours at a time of potential downtime. And that is only if the terrain remains the same, such as the rolling hills of the Midwest. Otherwise you can enjoy the changing scenery, etc.

There are so many things you can do within each two-hour block that time truly will fly. Breaking time down in this manner makes it very easy for families with small children to road-trip any distance, by having these smaller driving chunks for each day. Doing this method you can literally drive from one side of the United States to the other without conflict or exhaustion setting in. It's when fatigue, hunger and boredom sets in that issues arise; however, keep in mind that by following the roadtrip commandments everyone will stay comfortable and engaged.

Aside from being present and simply enjoying the ride, having introverted time for self-reflection or simply zoning out and listing to music, there is a list of activities to keep you engaged and truly enjoying every minute of a roadtrip. To take advantage of downtime you should do what you feel like and let things flow, but remember that "variety is the spice of life." Switch it up with some music if you're feeling reflective as you enjoy the landscape, an audiobook if you feel like learning, or even listen to a comedian if you are rolling across an endless terrain and simply want entertainment.

You can take a little time and send updates or photos to a friend or family member. If you are keeping a journal, be sure and capture your impressions from recent experiences. If you're with friends, you can follow the list of interactive questions later in this book to strengthen your relationships as you learn more about each other on a much deeper level (there are funny questions as well, such as your worst date experience, etc.). You can also see the games list which will provide interactive games for you all to play while driving. Downtime is also a great opportunity for research on either the next region coming up, to see if you want to stop anywhere interesting in two hours, or research on the final destination. You can look up the best restaurants or local food that you've got to try. For example, when in New Orleans you've gotta try the etouffee and jambalaya, or when in Southern Cali, fish tacos are a must. It's a great time to do some fun research and share with your fellow roadtrippers.

This guide includes many engaging activity ideas including games and questions listed by category—for couples, groups and families—but make sure you read through them all because some will apply universally. If you constantly change it up within each two-hour frame, the downtime flies by! It all depends on your mood; you just have to feel it out. An example of a full day's drive (8 hours) with different dynamics would be:

Block One (2 hours)

- Spend an hour listening to an audiobook.

- Reflect for an hour with some relaxing music in the background while enjoying the scenery.

- It's break time already! so pull over at an interesting stop within the next few minutes, or find a gas station for your break ritual. Go for a quick hike, explore for 20 minutes or simply jump back on the road.

Block Two (2 hours)

- Spend one hour asking the partner questions if you're driving with a partner, each taking your time and answering deeply, letting the conversation flow organically and lead to follow up questions.

- Play one hour of games (see game list).

- What?! Its time to pull over! Stop at the next local fruit stand for 20 minutes or anytime within this block when you come across something. Grab lunch and immerse yourself—try the local food! If you're driving through Texas, try some BBQ.

Block Three (2 hours)

- Use one hour to research the top restaurants or the creepiest ghost stories in the state you're in.

- Don't forget food! Don't eat out of boredom, but definitely take your time if you're enjoying those healthy snacks.

- Listen for 30 minutes to a YouTube video about your next destination

- Enjoy 30 minutes cruising to your best roadtrip music and enjoying the scenery and open road.

- Okay! It's break time already, so pull over at that shady little food truck and risk it. Enjoy!

Block Four (Final 2 hours)

- Take one hour for local music in the background as you and your crew share funny stories.

- Try taking an hour to google research on your next destination to build excitement or see where you can stop for your next two-hour stop coming up. (If you are the copilot you can do this and share with the driver.)

- Look! Break time already. Pull over at a bathroom because that shady food truck was a bad idea! Check into your hotel and enjoy the evening.

Advice on the Final Two-Hour Block

Regardless if you're driving three or four hours total to your final destination for that evening, or the full eight hours a day, stopping every two hours is always advised. Also, always try to use that last block to focus on and get excited about your destination. If you're solo, you can YouTube facts about the city and listen to it the last hour of the drive. I repeat, LISTEN to it, don't watch, and don't switch between videos while driving. By learning about your destination shortly before arriving it not only builds anticipation but allows you to appreciate the region and culture, motivating you to immerse yourself more.

As long as you have at least one passenger besides your dog, put them to work the last hour doing this research to discover the best things to anticipate ahead. Refer to the "Take Advantage of Technology" section. Your companion can navigate to a top restaurant or a must-see roadside attraction, like a giant pistachio statue in Arizona. Kidding—they better find something more interesting than that! Not only will you enjoy discovering these treasures to look forward to experiencing very soon, but you are less likely to miss out on anything worth checking out in the area as you pass through.

THE BREAK RITUAL

As mentioned in the 26 Roadtripping Commandments, the "break ritual" consists of a few quick exercises that you do after stopping every two hours. This stop can also be used for a bathroom break, food break, to walk a pet if you have one, to explore the area, to get a quick hike in, and for enjoying the unique qualities of the area you're passing through. These stops every two hours are crucial, not only for your well-being and keeping you alert, but they also force you to interact with the environment and truly experience each area. Also, it's important for your health to promote circulation and mobility which will also keep energy levels high.

Break Ritual Routine / A Universal Sign

1. Reaching overhead and leaning to the right and left

2. 10 rotations

3. 10 squats

4. 10 repetitions of calf raises

5. Hip flexor/ calf stretch

> Just think—one day you may pull over at a gas station and see fellow travelers get out of their dust-caked vehicles and start doing these exact exercises. When this happens say hello...you are obligated! In fact, watch for a universal sign of a fellow, like-minded roadtripper. If you see this universal sign—travelers getting out of their cars and starting to stretch their arms in the air in unison, followed by rotations, squats, calf raises, and a hip flexor stretch—looking like a roadside boot camp—say hello!

Help build the roadtrip community and make new friends, take a picture with your fellow roadtrippers as a group and hashtag #howtoroadtripamerica and #Roadtrippingfam and tag your location!

THE CHANGING DYNAMIC

A Solo Trip vs. Partner or Group

Traveling With Your Furry Friend

The dynamic of who comes along doesn't change the experiences necessarily; it just affects the planning process a little in most areas. You want to adjust how you pack, bringing more food and water, etc. while remaining mindful. Aside from this, everything else has similar planning.

CRUISIN' SOLO

First off, applaud yourself. Not everyone feels confident, comfortable, or independent enough to plan and take a roadtrip on their own; yet, it can be one of the most rewarding things you'll ever do. I strongly feel that everyone needs to try a roadtrip by themselves, regardless if you are more introverted or extroverted. A trip by yourself gives you a chance to relax, think both deeply and broadly, while giving perspectives on a different level. You will not only get to know yourself more deeply, you will also gain confidence as you rely on only yourself and do things outside of your comfort zone. These trips get you out of your old routines, expand your mind, and can truly be life-changing if you are open-minded.

Though you're alone, remember to stop every two hours to do the Break Ritual, which stretches your legs, wakes up your mind, and gets your circulation going. After the exercises, briefly check out the surrounding area and you can take a few minutes to research the upcoming area. It may be easy but don't overlook this! Trust me, you'll stay refreshed and alert by stopping every two hours, while taking advantage of this time to immerse yourself in your surroundings.

SOLO QUESTIONS

Make sure you read through the "Art of Being" (Chapter 16) for more insight on using a solo trip for self-growth. You have the unique opportunity to think deeply, and ask yourself key questions, and here is a list of questions/prompts you may find useful. Solo trips are the perfect time for self-discovery, so take advantage and go deep! Many of these are challenging to answer, so take your time and don't expect to be able to have instant answers to them all; you will learn over time. The value to you is in the inquiry, so don't struggle to find any perfect answers. I advise reading one at a time and thinking about it until the next stop—then you can go to the next. Avoid looking at the list while driving, for safety reasons.

1. What gives meaning to my life?

2. What gifts do I have?

3. What brings me joy?

4. What would my perfect day look like?

5. What am I passionate about?

6. Who needs the gifts I bring?

7. If money wasn't an issue, what would I do with my time?

8. What verb best describes me?

9. What problem in the world do I want to solve?

10. What do I wish I had more time to do?

11. Who means the most to me in my life?

12. What was my favorite thing to do as a kid?

13. When was the last time I felt lit up?

14. What kind of a person do I want to be in 5 years?

15. What allows me to lose track of time?

16. What am I drawn to?

17. What makes me smile?

18. If I could send a message to a large group of people, who would they be, and what would the message say?

19. What is on my bucket list?

20. What abilities did I have as a child?

21. What do I love to learn about?

22. If given one wish that cannot be used on myself, what would I wish for?

23. If I could start my career over, what would I do?

24. What does success mean to me right now?

25. Is there anyone I am holding back from telling something important about how I feel?

CRUISIN' WITH BAE

If you're feeling adventurous and want to take a trip with your sweetie-pie, hubby, wifey, pookie bear, sweetheart, babe, cuddle bug, darlin', honey bunny, pumpkin, sugar cube, or whoever the hell your significant other is, here are some notes to ensure the trip of a lifetime.

If it's your first roadtrip, uh-oh! No pressure! It's going to make or break your... Just playing—you're going to be fine regardless and this is only going to deepen your relationship. Nothing strengthens bonds as much as spending a lot of uninterrupted time together, especially outside of each other's comfort zones. A roadtrip will truly take things to another level, so before literally taking things to another level, consider a roadtrip! It will allow you to learn much more about your partner than you ever knew previously.

This applies across the board: If you just started dating your lil stud muffin or honey bun, and you want to see how well you work together before taking things to the next level...this is your chance! There is no better compatibility check than sharing a small space for long periods of time with no TV, no best friends dropping in, nor any absolutes on division of labor. How well you do when outside of your comfort zone, with someone you are just getting to know while they are outside of their comfort zone, makes for an interesting time, to say the least.

I definitely advise starting with a short trip, possibly a day trip and then an overnight trip before trying one for a few consecutive days or more. I'm not saying to judge your significant other based on a trip; there

Chapter 6: It's all about the journey

shouldn't ever be judgment and this should never be considered a test in your mind because that will not only put you in a negative mindset but will take away from your trip. That would absolutely dampen the entire adventure if you focus on analyzing each other in that sense. I simply mean, you will have time to ask deeper questions and to do things together that you normally would not and learn much more about each other. You will discover what each other finds exciting, scary, boring, maddening, funny, or ridiculous and you will truly appreciate each other on a much deeper level after. There are always challenges on a roadtrip, usually none too difficult, but you'll see how it works to problem-solve together. A roadtrip will show you how great you are for each other and you'll care for one another much more after, that's all. Of course this wouldn't be recommended for a second date, but if you are really moving fast and feel comfortable a month in and optimistic about being together, seize the opportunity for a day trip! Just having the common desire to take a roadtrip adventure together means a lot about your compatibility. Make sure you both use the Commandments of Roadtripping as a guideline, making sure to stop every two hours and switch drivers, if possible. (I know I keep repeating this, but some of you still need to recognize how important this is.)

Ways to take advantage of the downtime will be the same as a solo trip with additional options

- Listen to music and have quiet time to just reflect and enjoy the ride.

- Agree on or take turns selecting an audiobook or comedian to listen to.

- You can play games with each other.

- You can ask thoughtful questions from the list below and have deep conversations.

- Passenger can entertain the driver with google facts, trivia, or your destination's history.

30 Fun/Deep/Possibly Uncomfortable Partner Questions

Ask questions! Make sure you really listen to their responses and you can then elaborate on what they say and let that lead into natural follow-up questions. Remember the goal is not to get through a certain number of questions, but to have prompts that bring out what makes the other person who they are, letting a question trail into follow up questions and seeing where it takes you. The questions should encourage conversation and allow quality discussions that deepen your relationship. Some of these are fun, while some are deep and require more reflection, so take your time. If a question makes you uncomfortable, it is usually a good idea to dig deep and try to answer it; this is when the most growth will occur, not only within yourself but also in your relationship. Part of building a relationship is opening up and building connection and trust. Don't rush through them! Of course you must take turns—no one gets to only ask questions without also answering them.

1. What were your first thoughts when we met?

2. What would constitute a perfect day for you?

3. For what in your life do you feel the most grateful?

4. If you could wake up tomorrow and have gained one quality or ability, what would it be?

5. What is one rule for yourself that you will never break?

6. If you could change one thing about your childhood, what would it be?

7. What is the greatest accomplishment in your life?

8. What is our funniest memory together?

9. What do you value most in a friendship? And relationship?

Chapter 6: It's all about the journey

10. If you knew one year from now you would die, what would you change about the way you're living today?

11. If you knew you could accomplish anything, what would you attempt?

12. If we were to break up tomorrow, what would you miss the most?

13. When did you last sing to yourself?

14. Would you like to be famous? If so, why and for what?

15. Of anyone alive today or past, whom would you like to talk with over dinner?

16. What is something that nobody knows about you?

17. What have you always wanted to ask me?

18. In four minutes, tell me your life story in as much detail as possible, ready—go!

19. If I had to move to another planet for a year, would you wait for me or break up with me?

20. What frightens you the most when it comes to love?

21. What is your most treasured memory in general?

22. How is our relationship special?

23. Tell your partner three things that you admire about them.

24. How do you like to show your love?

25. What is your most embarrassing memory?

26. What physical aspect of me do you love the most?

27. If you were to die and not have the opportunity to tell someone something, what would it be? To whom? And why haven't you told them yet?

28. When did you last cry in front of someone? By yourself?

29. If your house was on fire and everyone was safely outside, but you had a moment for a final dash inside to grab one item, what would it be?

30. Name three strengths you see in your partner.

31. What would your ideal date be?

32. What was our favorite date and why?

33. What was the nicest thing you ever did for another person?

Partner Games

Three Levels Deep—Wave goodbye to your comfort zone. In this game, you and your partner each get only three questions (not ones from the previous questions list—those are too easy!) and you have to each answer, being 100% truthful. I'm sure you always are, regardless, but the entire point of this game is to ask three questions that you would never, ever ask otherwise. I could give examples, but you get the idea…be creative... and good luck!

Write a song inspired by your roadtrip—For example, if you're in Texas, put on some country acoustics and write lyrics together until you've got "it!" If you're proud of your song and think you should be famous, make a video singing it and tag us on social media! #howtoroadtripamerica #myroadtripsong

Storytelling—Take turns creating a story by switching authors after each line (or paragraph). When it's your turn, build on the existing story, but you can go in any direction you choose. Make it fun! In one version, you start the story using the name of the town or landmark you are passing at the time.

Car I.D.—Call out the make and model (and year, if you're awesome!) of every car on the road with you. Keep score to see who gets the most points (one per correct I.D.). Another version is to find as many cars as you can of the same model as one you have owned in the past. (Good for some "my first car…" stories!)

CREW CRUISIN'

Cruising with friends offers many benefits and changes the dynamic slightly to one of more activity and more conversation. There are more games that you can potentially play and conversations will naturally be longer. I know I keep reminding you, but make sure you stop every two hours and switch drivers so you can all stay fresh…even if you don't feel like it. The point is to never feel like you have to stop by not getting to that point!

Questions with Friends

Start with the driver and then go clockwise throughout your vehicle, taking turns—each person should answer the same question before moving to the next to keep everyone engaged and not miss out on some good answers!

1. Describe your worst first date ever and take turns.
2. What food would you never eat under any circumstances?
3. If you could go back in time, what year would you travel to?
4. If you could have been a child prodigy, what skill would you choose to have?
5. What was your favorite toy or game growing up?
6. Favorite food growing up?
7. What is the worst job you have ever had and why?

8. If you could stay a certain age forever, what age would it be?

9. If you could meet anyone living or dead, who would it be?

10. Would you want to know the exact date of your death? Why or why not?

11. If you could breed two completely different animals, what would they be and what would the new species be called?

12. Do you believe in ghosts? Why or why not?

13. Do you believe in Bigfoot? Why or why not?

14. Do you believe in extraterrestrials? Why or why not?

15. If you could learn one new skill by snapping your fingers, what would it be?

16. If you were to start a blog, what would it be about?

17. What is the one thing that keeps you up at night?

18. What is the biggest mistake in your life and why?

19. What is the best purchase you have ever made in your life and why? Biggest?

20. When you think of success, what comes to mind?

21. What do you value in a friendship?

22. Have you ever ignored one of my texts? Why?

23. What did you learn growing up that sticks with you today?

24. What was your childhood like?

25. Who was your role model when you were young?

26. What was the most romantic thing anyone has ever done for you?

27. If you could quit your job and do anything, what would it be?

28. What do you wish more people knew about you?

29. What would you do if you had an entire weekend open?

30. Do you consider yourself an expert on anything?

31. What was your best memory with each of us?

Games with Friends

While You Were Sleeping—This one takes advantage of sleepy passengers because they should have followed the roadtrip commandments and gotten rest the night before! Within this game, the non-sleeping passengers let the drowsy passenger fall asleep...for a minimum of 5 minutes... Then you start creating a story of what the sleeping passenger missed, each taking a turn adding a section. Once the passenger wakes up you have to get them to believe the story! If they are passed out, feel free to wake them up by saying, "You missed it!" and then start with your story. If anyone breaks character they lose one point. If you succeed in convincing them you all get 3 points, but if the passenger catches on, they get 3 points. The most points at the destination wins!

21 QUESTIONS—One roadtripper volunteers and the other passengers take turns asking the volunteer a question. You can't ask the same question twice and the volunteer can only pass on two questions. When the 21 are up, they pick who is next. Depending on the time before your next stop and other factors, you can play "10 Questions" vs. twenty-one.

Fortunately/Unfortunately—This game puts things in perspective by allowing you to see there is always good in even seemingly bad circumstances. One person starts by saying something has happened that was fortunate. The next person in turn has to say something *unfortunate* about the same thing the last person said was fortunate. Keep going until someone stumbles with the wrong start or takes more than three seconds to come up with the next part of the story. Then they are "out."

Example: One person begins, "Fortunately, we brought plenty of food." Next person: "Unfortunately, there's no more room in the cooler." Next person: "Fortunately, we haven't gotten lost…" There is no limit to creative starts for this game. "Fortunately, I found a fifty-dollar bill on the sidewalk…" or, "Fortunately, my friend from elementary school found me on Facebook…" or, "Fortunately, I inherited my mother's musical talent…"

Regional Food Master—Collect the most regional food items along your journey as possible from gas stations. At each gas station you must find one locally produced item—the hunt can provide surprising and humorous results, believe me. Memorable examples include gator jerky and spicy dried cacti. Whoever has the most examples wins at the end of the trip, and duplicate items don't count.

The Counting Game—Seems simple, as one random person calls out "1" and everyone tries to count out loud collectively to reach 20. If two or more people start to say the same number at the same time, you pause for 5 seconds and start over.

Battle of the Bands—Two aspiring DJs compete while the other passengers give the challenges, such as "best classic rock song" or "best song about roadtrips." The two competitors take turns playing their selection via their smartphone and the others vote. Creative challenges include using the state or region you are in: "Best song with 'California' in the lyrics," for example, or challenge the DJs to see who can come up with the most songs containing a place found on your roadtrip.

Word Association—One person begins with a word and you all take turns giving related words, and the game continues until someone messes up and says something unrelated. Keep in mind the words don't have to be synonyms, but simply related, such as: beach, towel, water, sun, bikini, island, Cuba, cigar, and so forth.

Cows on My Side!—When there are cows on your side of the road, you call out, "Cows on my side!" and get one point. Likewise, the person on the opposite side does the same, and the winner is whoever has the most points when you reach the next stop. (Loser buys the snacks!)

CRUISIN' WITH THE FAM

This section is all about you and your family, regardless of your children's ages. Though an upcoming book in this series will focus on families and provide more in-depth information on how to best take a roadtrip with your family, this chapter will give you a great start. I list an array of things to keep your kids busy and enjoying the open road. First off, as long as you're stopping at places you see along the way, every two hours your kids or fellow passengers will stay more engaged with what is going on, and you'll all be looking for interesting places to stop when driving through small cities, etc.

1. Use audible or audiobooks that will interest your kids. If you put on a Harry Potter series for one hour, it's flown by before you know it. This is also a golden opportunity to share a childhood favorite of your own, something they have not been exposed to before.

2. Create kids' playlists for songs that they like (I use "Spotify") and you can resort back to this playlist in times of need. Rather than just including the same songs they listen to all the time, liberally sprinkle in roadtrip songs like "I've Been Everywhere" by Johnny Cash, "On the Road Again" by Willie Nelson, "Route 66" by Chuck Berry, or "Take it Easy" by the Eagles. By the end of the trip you may find yourself all singing together.

3. Movies: Of course you can resort to movies, but don't let old familiar habits overtake the unique opportunities of traveling together. Especially for older kids, skip the movies and encourage interactive games, question exchange and sing-alongs. A movie can be a last resort and you can simply use your mobile device, strategically placed to make your car into a movie theater for the passengers.

An example block of a full day of roadtripping with your family might look like this: 500 miles or eight hours, and let's say you're driving from Tampa, Florida, to Atlanta, Georgia, and spending the night there. I wouldn't set anything in a rigid schedule; rather, let the following happen naturally when everyone wants to participate in each activity, or plan general details before so you have stops set up.

Eight hours broken down in two-hour blocks is only four driving blocks. If you have another driver with you, then switch after each two-hour driving block and you get to stay nice and refreshed. Keep in mind this is the maximum recommended driving distance in a day! Each of you will only drive two, two-hour blocks...easy! It really puts it in perspective to examine the time and distance relationship in this way.

It's literally the equivalent of driving from Sarasota, Florida, to Orlando, Florida, taking a break and then doing whatever you want for a couple of hours (while the other person drives, in this example) before you drive your last 2-hour block. Then spend the final two hours relaxing and doing whatever you want and getting excited about your arrival—while enjoying each part of that easy process. You'll be surprised at how easily you can drive 500 miles with two people and not even feel fatigued.

Block 1 = Leaving by 8am and driving the first two-hour block till 10am = regular conversation about the trip.

- Break, explore something, stretch your legs, have breakfast somewhere, look ahead at what to expect on the next stretch of road.

Block 2 = Back on the road by 11am and driving to 1pm = Games for an hour, one hour audio book (maybe a novel that interests your kids).

- Break time! Stop at a gas station or local park, go for a quick 20 minute hike or stop by a fruit stand and try local produce from Northern Florida!

Block 3 = Back on the road by 1:30pm and driving till 3:30pm.= Enjoy interactive questions for an hour. Research the surrounding area and what is to expect for an hour.

- Break, stop and have some southern food after stretching your legs, then check out a historic site for a bit.

Block 4 = Back on the road by 4:30 and driving to reach your destination by 6:30. Maybe a movie this last block or road trip music for an hour and time to yourself.

Look! You're there! See how easy a day of driving can be? Now to put that into perspective, take a 2,000 mile roadtrip and that can be broken down into four days of driving 500 miles a day, which translates into the general eight-hour driving schedule that was just displayed. Starting in the morning, enjoying a full day of activities with the crew, and then arriving by no later than 6:30pm to have the whole rest of the evening together to relax and unwind. Any length roadtrip can be broken down in this same manner and by doing so you can prevent yourself from getting tired on long trips. This is especially important to follow with younger children.

List of Questions for Family

These questions not only encourage children to look within and discover more about themselves, but they also strengthen relationships among all family members:

1. If you could only eat one food for the rest of your life, what would it be?

2. What has happened recently that you will remember for years?

3. What is your favorite memory you have had with us as a family?

4. What is your favorite memory with each family member individually?

5. What would your perfect day look like?

6. If you could live anywhere for three months, where would it be?

7. What was the nicest thing you ever did for someone else?

8. What is your proudest accomplishment?

9. What makes you feel loved?

10. What makes you feel brave?

11. If your stuffed animals or toys could talk, what would they say?

12. Pretend you're a chef, what would you serve at your restaurant?

13. If you were outside for an entire day, what would you do?

14. What three strengths do you feel you have?

15. What is the craziest thing you have eaten?

16. If you gave everyone in the family new names, what would they be?

17. What is something I always say to you?

18. What car are you going to drive when you grow up?

19. What do you want to be when you grow up?

FAMILY GAMES

Would You Rather—A question game that involves asking comparison questions that require you to think differently. Feel free to come up with your own as these are just meant to get you going:

- Would you rather have to sing every word you say or say out loud every word you read?

Chapter 6: It's all about the journey

- Would you rather be a famous director or famous actor?

- Would you rather eat peanut butter and jelly or pizza if you were on a desert island and could only choose one of those two?

- Would you rather live without internet or air conditioner and heat?

- Would you rather only use search engines online or social media?

- If you had to choose between being a lion or a monkey, which would you rather be and why?

- Would you rather only use a fork or only use a spoon?

- Would you rather be famous and ridiculed or average?

- Would you rather only have extremely spicy food or bland?

CRUISIN' WITH YOUR FURRY FRIEND

First off, I apologize if this chapter title excludes your little sidekick who has *no* fur—perhaps a hairless cat, an iguana, parrot, box turtle, or goldfish—the following tips are most applicable to dogs and cats.

When planning to travel with a pet, you need to think ahead. One thing you will definitely want to have is a window shade/screen (or two). You'll find these very valuable when driving in hot climates. Then you'll need to consult with each furry friend and put together their "pet pack." I recommend bringing the following items and placing them behind the passenger seat for easy access if you're a solo driver—or behind the driver seat if there will be a front-seat passenger for them to access easily. BE SURE there is a barrier between the seat and your items to prevent them (or anything back there!) from rolling up under the seats(s) into the front floor area (though the front seats of most cars don't allow anything to move under them, just be conscious of placement.).

If there are backseat passengers, you may keep the pet pack in the trunk, but you'll need to offer your furry buddy water and a bathroom break at each of your two-hour stops. PLEASE take the time to put their leash on BEFORE letting them out of the vehicle for any reason. This goes for both dogs and cats (I don't think I've ever seen a cat on a leash but they do tend to do their own thing so it seems like a good idea!).

Pet Pack List:

- Water bowl
- Food bowl
- Food bag
- Doggy litter bags
- Cat litter and scooper
- Blanket
- Gallon of water
- Chew toys

Looking After Your Furry Friend

This might seem like common sense to some, but here is a checklist when traveling with your pet:

1. Always check the backseat temperature once you get moving; in many cars, the only air conditioning vents are located low or at the bottom of the center console and oftentimes you may have an item which is blocking this. Always reach back and feel the temperature and your furry friend to make sure they aren't too hot, because in direct sunlight the backseat can still get very hot if those factors are present.

2. It's nice to have the window partly open for your furry friend while cruising at low speeds but if you do, lock the controls! Make sure the backseat window lock is ON so only you can control the window movement. This will prevent your pet from stepping on the window button and either opening it too far (if they're jumpers) or getting injured by closing it on themselves.

3. When you stop for each two-hour break, attach a leash while the pet is still in the car and then give them a brief walk, bathroom break, and offer water.

4. Never leave your pet in a hot car, even with windows cracked open, unless it is very cool out and it's just for minutes. You may have time to run into the convenience store, depending on the climate, but the best option is to have a spare key to keep the air-conditioned car running while still being able to lock it (works on most vehicles). This is best for safety reasons as well since you never want to leave everything you have unattended in a strange place, even for a minute—don't risk it.

5. Make sure your pet is never in direct sunlight when in the backseat in hot climates. The sun angle changes so check (again) and put up a window shade when you stop for your break, if needed.

6. Have an idea of pet-friendly hotels in the area of each destination.

Five Pet-Friendly Hotels

I've had good luck finding places that welcome pets; there are certainly more of them these days than there were a couple decades ago. Personally I have found the following to be the best, but you can always call and ask if the hotel is pet-friendly and, if so, what the pet fee is—though often the pet fee can be almost as much as the room itself! These are some I'm fond of, but pet policies can differ by region, so always call to find out what is offered where you wish to stay:

1. La Quinta—With over 900 hotels spread across 48 states, they are generally affordable and consistent in quality. Many locations do not charge a pet fee, though some near major highways now charge $20. As of this writing, there are only 11 locations that are not pet-friendly with five being in NYC, two in California, three in Texas and one in Kentucky.

2. Red Roof Inn—They apparently LOVE pets. With over 500 hotels in 36 states, they are all pet-friendly (except a few in NYC). In fact, you actually get a 10% discount when you bring your pet!

3. Best Western—All across North America, 1,600 (out of 2,000) of these hotels are pet-friendly. In my experience, they allow up to two dogs in a room, but make sure you call and ask about the pet policy for any particular location.

4. Aloft Hotel—With 104 pet-friendly properties in major cities, it can be a nice change from a typical hotel chain, though sometimes a little pricier. Their policies vary location by location, so you'll need to check to be sure.

5. Motel 6—There is often a negative association with motels (vs. hotels) since they are usually cheaper; however, this is a solid brand that you will find in even the smallest cities, with over 1,200 locations across the US. If you find yourself in the middle of nowhere with your pet, keep these in mind.

TAKING ADVANTAGE OF TECHNOLOGY

There are mobile apps for everything!

As mentioned in Commandment #26, keep phone use to a minimum. Think of it as a tool to take out and use when necessary for a purpose. I suggest generally avoiding social media platforms until the very end of your trip and then you can post photos, etc. It's easy to let the internet and social media become distracting.. In one study, 49% of vacationers felt that social media took away from their trip, while 17% felt frustrated with their partner's use of social media when on the trip! Yet, you definitely want to have and use a smartphone, and I'll explain how to do this so that it enhances your experience rather than taking away from your or your companions' enjoyment.

First, have this talk up front with your roadtrip companions so everyone is in agreement. Nothing kills the roadtrip vibe and point of the trip faster than passengers being on their phones, zoned out in the wrong way. In my experience, one legitimate reason to be on your phone is to use an app to assist you in a task related to your roadtrip (more about these to follow). Also, you may want to research something to share with your travel buddies about the surrounding area or upcoming destination. Simply live in the moment and learn to use technology to enhance your experience. New apps come out all the time, but here are ones I currently find useful:

AIRBNB

This company was started by a couple of guys in San Francisco who blew up an air mattress in their living room and started offering "bed and breakfast." Now they operate a global online marketplace accessible via their website or mobile app. You can find a privately-owned room, guest house, full home, or boutique hotel in areas all over the country, especially those which typically attract tourists. It is not designed for last-minute bookings, though you can try it, but the best idea is to use it during your pre-trip planning. There is usually something special about these lodgings, which can be a nice break from typical cheap hotels. For example, a friend booked a lakeside guest house using Airbnb which included use of kayaks and paddleboards and a full breakfast served by the owner in the main house, and paid the same as a nearby nice hotel would charge.

AROUNDME

AroundMe is a mobile app for iOS, Android, and Windows phone platforms that allows users to quickly find nearby Points of Interest (POI) such as restaurants, hotels, theaters, parking, hospitals and much more. AroundMe uses the built-in smartphone navigation capabilities to perform location-aware searches.

AUDIBLE

This app allows you listen to a professional narrator (or sometimes the author) read any kind of book you are in the mood for. Music is great, but audible can be better. Take advantage of some of the downtime and read a book…learn something! Knowledge is truly power. I recommend nonfiction books that are self-help such as business classics, but it's just preference on this one. You can always do a novel or short story collection.

Audible is a subscription service through Amazon, but if you are already a Prime member, you do not have to be a subscriber to listen for FREE to a wide variety of audio books (a rotating list, not just any book you want).

FACEBOOK

I highly advise avoiding any social media platforms because they can suck you in and take away from the moment, but they can be a useful tool IF you are using them for a specific and necessary purpose related to your travels. For example, if you find yourself in need of personal recommendations, you can quickly and easily connect with your large network of family and friends.

Here's a funny story. I personally have used Facebook to find friends who would come to my rescue after getting stuck in the mud in my old Land Rover Discovery when I tried to show my off-roading skills off at the end of a date...and then had to walk her home in the rain (never try to show off!). A post on FB generally has a wider reach than the contacts in your phone, and it wasn't long before two old friends from high school came to my rescue after I had walked her home!

You could potentially post a question for the best burgers in Seattle, or the best campsites in St. Augustine and chances are somebody in your network knows the answer. It can be more fun and give you more confidence when you are getting ideas from people you know vs. some internet site. However, there is a time and place for this, the best time being prior to your trip as you do your research and planning. Don't try to refer to FB for every question you have because you'll begin to become too engaged with it as everyone responds to every question.

I know, it's a hard habit to break! But, my mission is to advise you on the BEST way to roadtrip, and using social media is just not advisable except for quick posts throughout to share the journey with friends and family, for certain needs, or creating an album after.

I do advise using Facebook to document your travels for yourself and of course so family and close friends can get the details of your adventures. I always recommend creating an album with the title of your adventure and begin in a timeline fashion, starting with photos of packing and leaving on Day One. Include a photo of each type of terrain along your journey, food experiences, local signs, and so forth—anything that is memory-provoking. I know there are people who will hate you if you post food photos, but these memories are for you to enjoy later, and many times the meal image itself will help you reminisce about the places you enjoyed the most and the ones you want to include in a future return trip. I personally like to write good Yelp reviews on places that I enjoyed which allows me to keep track of any type of business that I want to return to next time im in the area again.

I suggest this activity at the very end of the trip when you're almost home, within an hour or two of being home and you're not driving, or once you get home. By doing this the final hour or two, you can have fun going through pictures with your friends and choosing the order, while laughing about certain experiences. It's a great way to end the trip. Keep in mind not to begin too soon though, because the trip home is still a part of your trip that needs to be enjoyed! I'd save it for within two hours of being home or after you arrive.

GAS BUDDY

Should I stop here for gas? It seems a little on the expensive side... The GasBuddy app is a GPS-based application program for smartphones and tablets which provides prices of nearby gas stations from user-submitted data, as well as through partnerships with other companies and directly from station operators. The app has Android, BlackBerry 10, and iOS versions.

HOTEL TONIGHT

This app will save you from being homeless on the road! It allows you to find discounted hotel rooms (last minute deals) in your area. Rather than check individual hotels one by one, the app gives you the summary of what is currently available. With literally 2 or 3 clicks, you can have your room booked!

INSTAGRAM

You can post pictures along your journey and use hashtags appropriately. Doing this not only shares your experiences with friends and family, but also create a timeline for you to reflect on when you later review your travels. The hashtags can connect you to other travelers who visited the same or similar areas. It's a great app, but do this at the right time! Do not let Instagram, Pinterest, SnapChat, or ANY social media draw you in to their mazes where you can get lost and miss out on the journey.

NAVIGATION

This app comes with your iPhone but another variation is Waze. These are necessary for trips as they guide you and allow you to zoom out to see cities along your route. Finding large cities along your route allows you to not only take the name of that city and search what it offers on Yelp (as mentioned previously), but also attractions, etc. if the trip is an unplanned one. Keep in mind that sometimes you'll lose service and won't be able to restart this app for directions. If you're in a desolate area, keep the app running to keep it working despite the lack of a signal, or worst case you can even typically use it as a live map by zooming in and referencing the blue location dot with the map even without service.

SPOTIFY

Music makes a huge difference, as I mentioned earlier, especially listening to the music of the local area, or otherwise related to what you are doing. Such themes include songs of the season such as "summertime" or "Christmas" or "winter wonderland." You don't have to jam out to these all the time, but try to appreciate "theme music" while checking out attractions, etc., as it enriches the experience.

With the Spotify app, you can choose a tune such as a Christmas song, create a playlist, and then add a few more. You'll then automatically get some similar-type recommendations at the bottom of the newly created playlist, making your task of building a full playlist much easier. (In a later section, we'll discuss much more about music and playlists.)

TRIPADVISOR

This is the largest "social travel website" in the world, with about 315 million reviewers (active and inactive) and about 500 million reviews of hotels, restaurants, attractions and other travel-related businesses. TripAdvisor was an early adopter of user-generated content—the website services are free to users, who provide most of the content.

VENMO

If you're traveling with others, this app will make it simple and easy to split costs anytime, anywhere! Transfers are immediate and appear right in your bank account seconds after being submitted, and you can send anyone any amount of money.

YELP

As I touched on previously, this app can help you track your favorite places in each city. If you loved a particular park, attraction, or restaurant, write a review and also take a picture to add as well. Write the review on why you loved the establishment and include the city. Then you can go back and scan through your reviews to find past favorites in each city. It can also help you find recommendations (or warnings!) for anything you want in your area, especially when it comes time to get some food. If you're the passenger while in transit, you can search the surrounding area or use it in collaboration with the navigation app to search what the next city has to offer.

YOUTUBE

We think of YouTube for watching videos, but also drivers can utilize the app for listening to recommendations about an area you are approaching, for example. Instead of having to read online reviews or information, you can get someone on YouTube to tell you everything while you listen and drive. Generally, any major city will have a "must sees" video on YouTube.

There is a nearly infinite array of worthwhile listening experiences on YouTube, from TED talks to famous speeches to hilarious comedy routines. Most any subject or question you may think to "google" is probably available in video/audio form on YouTube.

Music

It's all about the playlists!

The music you listen to will drastically enhance your experiences! For example, imagine going to the gym and working out in silence, or even a group workout class without music! Now in regards to experiences, imagine listening to Tupac or old school hip hop while driving through a winter wonderland environment such as South Lake Tahoe in mid-December...It would be hard to get into the Christmas spirit with music that doesn't match the experience. Use music to enhance your experience! Now picture the same experience with Christmas music or something more fitting and you can see the drastic difference.

The need for music is ingrained in us, it has the power to influence emotions and bring on certain feelings.

Music is not only entertaining, it has many psychological benefits that can directly influence your mood and thoughts, relax the mind and body, and boost energy. However, in more depth, different types of music have benefits that vary; music with a slower tempo tends to help with memory retention, while upbeat music tends to increase processing speed. Instrumentals or classical music tend to have the best effect on mental performance (if studying, for example) because songs with lyrics tend to be more distracting as you process the words throughout each song. Music directly impacts a person's autonomic nervous system and allows listeners to recover more quickly from stressors.

FREE MUSIC RESOURCES

Finding free music (other than your AM/FM radio) is a lot easier than it used to be. You can find pretty much any song you want using just a few apps. Some of the best legal, free music apps are:

- iHeartRadio. Price: Free
- Jango Radio. Price: Free
- Pandora Music. Price: Free / $4.99-$9.99 per month
- Slacker Radio. Price: Free / $3.99 per month / $9.99 per month
- SoundCloud. Price: Free / $9.99 per month.
- Spotify. Price: Free / $9.99 per month
- TuneIn Radio. Price: Free / $9.99.
- YouTube. Price: Free / $13.99 per month

Regardless of what you listen to, it has its own benefits. It can put you into a different mindset to better immerse yourself in the surrounding area and enjoy the present. I always recommend using the mobile app, Spotify, and local radio stations if you want to not only see the area you're in, but hear and feel the vibe of it, the people, and culture. You can use pre-made playlists as well to enrich your experience of an area by listening to themed music (cowboy songs for cowboy country, and so forth).

As I mentioned in the "Taking Advantage of Technology" section, Spotify is great and is well worth purchasing the premium version, if only to cover the duration of your roadtrip. If you don't want to keep it (for $9.99/month), you can go back to the free version after your trip. I definitely recommend creating various playlists prior to your trip. These playlists can and should vary greatly—from your favorite songs within each genre, to roadtrip classics, music that you know gives you energy and motivation to drive, and music that you think fits the region within each part of your trip. Spotify is great to use for this because there will be many times that you don't have cellular internet service available, yet you can have the playlist downloaded and not be affected, or the app simply plays on its own regardless.

Get creative and use music to enhance the mood or experience—if you're driving through Texas, give country music a try for at least a little while, just like you would try the local BBQ. This will immerse you in the culture and put you in that mindset to better appreciate what the region has to offer.

Remember, the entire point of a roadtrip is to be spontaneous and enjoy the journey and in order to do so, you must truly immerse yourself into each region, far beyond your comfort zone. If you leave your home city and eat your usual foods, listen to the same music, and do the same activities, then you're simply bringing everything with you! Your experience is what you make of it and the more you immerse yourself the better it will be.

The joy in these trips is to LIVE IT! See each region as an opportunity—maybe a once-in-a-lifetime opportunity…who knows if you'll ever drive through a particular town in Alabama again? (Play "Sweet Home Alabama" by Lynyrd Skynyrd as you drive down a country back road.) To put this in perspective with another similar example, imagine you are about to drive through an old ghost town in Arizona. Wouldn't it be distracting if Limp Bizkit is playing in the background? As I mentioned earlier, music will always either complement or distract from each experience. As you are waiting in anticipation of your roadtrip, work on building different playlists. You can do it on your own or build it with a partner or friends.

Title your playlists whatever you want and add songs to each one prior to each trip within each category. It can be fun to do with a partner or friends as you use the recommended songs and go through to determine which ones to add to build a great playlist. Here are some ideas from my personal playlists on Spotify (for free access to many of my pre-made playlists within each genre, follow Jonathansimos on Spotify). Here are some recommendations within certain categories to get you started:

Roadtrip Classics

- Bachman-Turner Overdrive, "Takin' Care of Business" and "Roll On Down the Highway"
- Buffalo Springfield, "For What It's Worth"
- Canned Heat, "Going up the Country"
- Chuck Berry, "Route 66"
- Citizen Cope, Carlos Santana, "Son's Gonna Rise"
- Counting Crows, "Mr. Jones"
- Eagles, "Take It Easy"
- Johnny Cash, "I've been Everywhere" and "Ring of Fire"
- Kansas, "Carry Onward Wayward Son"
- Kid Rock, "All Summer Long"
- Lynyrd Skynyrd, "Sweet Home Alabama"
- Norman Greenbaum, "Spirit in the Sky"
- Red Hot Chili Peppers, "Road Trippin'"
- The Allman Brothers Band, "Midnight Rider"
- The Band, "Atlantic City"
- The Beatles, "Drive my Car"
- The Temper Trap, "Sweet Disposition"
- Tom Cochrane, "Life is a Highway"
- Tom Petty, "Free Fallin'"

Just Cruising

- Aloe Blacc, "Wake Me Up"
- Bastille, "Pompeii"
- Bon Iver, "Blood Band"
- Bon Iver, "Holocene"
- Bon Iver, "Skinny Love"
- Dan + Shay, "Tequila"
- Duke Dumont, "Ocean Drive"
- Ed Sheeren, "Give Me Love"
- Grizfolk, "In My Arms"
- Hozier, "From Eden"
- James Bay, "Hold Back the River"
- James Bay, "Let it Go"
- James Blake, "I Need a Forest Fire"
- Kaleo, "All the Pretty Girls"
- Kaleo, "Way Down We Go"
- Lauv, "I Like Me Better"
- Marshmello "Silence"
- Marshmello, "Happier"
- Milky Chance, "Flashed Junk Mind"
- Milky Chance, "Stolen Dance"
- Mumford and Sons, "The Cave"
- Mumford and Sons, "There Will Be Time"
- Niall Horan, "Slow Hands"
- Robin Schultz, "Oh Child"
- The Head and the Heart, "All We Ever Knew"
- The Lumineers, "Ophelia"
- Vance Joy, "Fire and the Flood"

Chapter 6: It's all about the journey

- Vance Joy, "Georgia"
- Vance Joy, "Mess is Mine"
- X Ambassadors, "Renegades"
- X Ambassadors, "Kerosene Dreams"
- X Ambassadors, "Unsteady"

Upbeat Classical

- Black Violin, "A-Flat"
- Black Violin, "Opus"
- Black Violin, "Shaker"
- Black Violin, "Virtuoso"
- Black Violin, "Vivaldi"
- Bond, "Pump It"
- Damien Escobar, "Am I Wrong"
- Lindsey Sterling, "Crystallize"
- Lindsey Sterling, "Song of a Caged Bird"
- Lindsey Sterling, "Stars Align"
- Lindsey Sterling, "Where Do We Go"

Zooming Along

- DJ Snake, "Magenta Riddim"
- Dynoro, "In My Mind"
- Major Lazer, "Believer"
- Major Lazer, "Light it up"
- Major Lazer, DJ Snake, "Lean On"
- Marshmello "Together"
- Panjabi MC, "Beware of the Boys"
- Prismo, "Senses"

- Prismo, "Too Close"
- Wide Awake, "Ready"
- Willy William, "La La La"

Other Sample Category Ideas

- American classics
- California reggae
- Christmas music
- Country
- Disney
- Fall music
- Folk songs
- Old-school hip hop
- Reggae
- Reggaeton
- Theme music
- Funny songs
- Slow songs/R&B
- etc...

Chapter 6: It's all about the journey

Eating potato chips on potato chip rock near San Diego, California

PART 2

"All you need to know is that it's possible."

– "Wolf," Appalachian Trail Hiker

Chapter 7

CHOOSE YOUR OWN ADVENTURE

Overview of trip types, setting the foundation of your journey

The widest trees in the world, Sequoia National Park, California

YOUR TRIP FOUNDATION

Like anything else in life, it's best to know generally what you want, your purpose. I have simplified the roadtrip planning process to make it as efficient as possible for travelers, so you simply have to go through a total of eight quick base steps which can be done in minutes and leave you with a dream adventure. These eight crucial steps will be listed shortly, after an overview. It is important to understand that every single roadtrip simply breaks down into three main parts:

1. Roadtrips will always be one of three trip styles. Destination based/ Experienced based/ or Travel based

2. Every roadtrip style will be either Planned or Unplanned. This simply sets a range for the level of pre-determined details, from the bare minimum but necessary, to highly-detailed but not overdone. Regardless of which trip type listed above, it will ultimately be either generally Unplanned (a more spontaneous trip) or Planned (more details planned out rather than just the base steps).

3. They should have an underlying Theme. There can and should always be an underlying theme for your roadtrips, as they make it more fun and allow you to know what experiences to seek overall.

An overview, before going in depth

If you plan too little, the trip can be more stressful than enjoyable; yet, if you plan every fine detail, there is little room to enjoy the process and whatever comes your way. Too much structure makes everything too rigid while not enough makes chaos; **balance is key**. That is exactly the purpose of this book, to guide you with the roadtrip commandments and simplify the roadtrip planning process with this breakdown, allowing you to build a trip foundation in just minutes and then either build on it further or just take off and get going!

Generally you will choose what you're most attracted to, perhaps trying one trip leaning to the left, being less planned but still having the fundamental base questions answered, while the other would lean more

Chapter 7: Choose your own adventure

to the right with more details planned, though it also begins with the base questions. The base questions simply provide that foundation for you to build upon while ensuring you have just the right amount of details and take it either way.

> ***Planning the ultimate roadtrip lies within a balance of
> just enough structure to allow direction
> and more of the experiences that you seek,
> while not being too planned or structured
> to allow the spontaneity of what the open road brings.***

TRIP TYPE
Destination, Experience or Travel Based?

Every roadtrip you take will either be destination-based, experience-based or travel-based. With the first type, you have a destination in mind from the onset and generally a reason to be there at a certain time (though not always the case). You probably have a predetermined arrival date as well, such as getting to the first day of Mardi Gras in New Orleans or driving to Tennessee for your friend's bachelorette or bachelor party. For a destination-based trip, you simply design a roadtrip around the event you are driving to that destination for.

An experience-based trip is when you simply want to take a roadtrip and do not need to be at a certain place by a certain date and time. You don't usually have a destination in mind initially, and the trip is planned with the focus being on what you want to experience. You planned this trip because you wanted to take a roadtrip and experience the local countryside or are in search of fall colors, or to go skiing wherever the first snow falls within your range. You simply wanted to *experience* the open road along with your surroundings and see what you happen to discover along the way. For this type, it generally comes down to how long you have and what you want to experience (this comes later in more depth.)

Travel-based would simply be a trip that doesn't typically have a timeframe and continues from city to city without a final destination. Generally spending the same amount of time in each city, this kind of trip is characterized by continuous travel for a longer period of time; a tour in a sense.

All of these trip types will be discussed in depth in the next three chapters, and understanding them will guide you on how to plan your ultimate trip.

The final part of the breakdown is Theme. This also will be discussed in more depth, though theme is generally icing on the cake in a sense where it makes your trips more fun and gives more clarity for what you want to experience. Theme gives each trip type more purpose and allows you to enjoy the little things more.

PLANNED AND UNPLANNED TRIPS

Determining the level of details and spontaneity

As I mentioned, all trips will be destination-based, experience-based, or travel-based; however, they are also all either planned or unplanned, with a theme thrown in. You will understand the importance of staying within these parameters after seeing an example: Imagine literally just packing up, jumping in the car, and driving north without any general destination in mind and only a vague idea of a time frame. I tried this, once. Sounds fun, but it is far from ideal.

Without knowing an ultimate destination, it is impossible to know how to pack for weather or activities, and you'll often be underprepared and spend most of your time and energy simply trying to bring everything together and plan your next move. Basically, you'll spend all your time and energy on open road survival, rather than adventure, activities and enjoyment. You can have the same excitement from spontaneity when you have what you need and some direction, both created in the base steps.

Without knowing at least the base steps, you don't know what key experiences you really want or what is in the area to strive for, nor can you figure out where to stop each day to see the best attractions in each area. You would miss key experiences, special moments, and memories. On a smaller scale, to put this in perspective, imagine wanting to go out on a Saturday without any direction or decisions made whatsoever. You would leave your house in pajamas and end up in a parking lot or local mall, drifting around your city like an unanchored ship.

You must have the base steps done regardless of the trip type, which is why there are base questions that you must ask yourself. They provide a secure structure to encompass everything you want across the spectrum! Then, if you end up feeling spontaneous and choose an unplanned trip, the necessary framework is there regardless. With an unplanned trip, you're able to have everything you need, knowing your general timeline and general areas in which to stop each evening, easing any stress while leaving you to be completely spontaneous to take any route that general direction. Stop or stay wherever you want last minute because, basically, you are safe to wing it from there!

To put it in perspective, let's look at the breakdown of a completely unplanned trip. Of course this is an extreme and ugly example, but you will get the distinction.

So in this extreme example where you don't answer the base questions and just jump in the car and head north, you have not had the pleasure of anticipating your upcoming trip, researching and considering what would make it most enjoyable for you, whether tightly planned or loosely structured. Now you are behind the wheel but there still is not much feeling of anticipation because you don't have any idea of what to expect! This anticipation is instead replaced by the discomfort of not knowing any consecutive steps—how long you should drive, what to look for in terms of landmarks, attractions, or experiences, where to potentially stay, etc. This type of trip is bound to be more stressful than enjoyable.

A variation of this trip would be one where you simply know the destination and nothing else in between. You may as well be on a train because you will miss so many experiences and discoveries along the journey. So always answer the base steps! The base will guide you and then allow you to choose your level of spontaneity.

To fully maximize a trip, you don't have to know every detail or plan everything, but it is a balance that either leans one way or the other. It comes down to one of two options, though each has the same base.

An example of the other extreme would be a trip where everything is planned. I can't stand the thought of taking a trip on a guided tour bus as I'm afraid everything would be on a set agenda, down to how many minutes I can stand on an overlook, sit in a diner, or stare at a grazing bison family. Too much structure and clock-watching is not for me. Being too planned will not only put unnecessary obligations and expectations on each travel member and causes stress, but also takes away from the bulk of the benefits of finding and seeking out the unknown along your journey. It puts you into a more mission-oriented mindset in order to accomplish your checklist. I don't think your mind realizes you are no longer at the office. You're still in work mode and can't fully relax. You may overlook many experiences that could otherwise be enjoyable and memorable. With that being said, the base steps create the boundaries in planning, so you can relax and don't have to worry about these extremes.

It is important to go through the steps with your travel mates so you all are also on the same page. If someone wants to plan every little detail from the exact time of arrival to every restaurant stop, with hotels booked in advance and each activity planned in different time slots each day, you would find this out in the initial planning and can get on the same page. Therefore, the base steps also get everyone in agreement with what they had in mind for the trip, and it generally paints the picture of what to expect.

I do recommend that everyone experience **both** types of trips within the framework I provide by doing the base steps, depending on how you are feeling around the time you begin to plan the trip. If you are in a highly structured job with almost no free time, you absolutely should consider an "unplanned trip" to give yourself a true break and rejuvenating experience. It is great for you to be as spontaneous as possible while having enough of a framework to prevent any stress and just allow you to enjoy your journey. Be willing to switch it up and try both trip types, depending on how you feel.

THEME IS YOUR "WHY"

We often have expectations for vacations, and when the trips don't live up to those expectations, we get disappointed. The key is not to have expectations but, rather, to know what you want to experience and seek to experience these things with an open mind. You want to have a general vision of the trip which your theme will provide.

Creating a theme offers more of what you desire for that trip, it allows you to know what to seek within your research for your trip. Your *theme* is your *why* and allows you to group more potential experiences together for what you want to experience. It is human nature to crave a sense of purpose and a theme enhances that.

The theme is your trip title.

For example: You have a friend's wedding in Vegas. This will be a destination-based trip but, of course, you still get to add a theme. You can call it: "What happens in Vegas, Stays in Vegas!" (I know it's cliché, but it certainly provides perspective). With this title, naturally it makes you want to experience all that Vegas has to offer! On the contrary, imagine you didn't give it a theme…it would not be as official and you may not feel as motivated to pursue these experiences. Theme gives more clarity and gives you a subtle sense of purpose to live the trip up while having an open mind.

Another example: You want to take a trip to go camping in the mountains with friends. This will be an experienced-based trip which you can call: "Epic Camping Trip." This sets the stage that you want to experience outdoor activities, camping, s'mores, campfires, hot chocolate, etc., rather than just saying you're going camping with friends. Do you see the difference?

The small title simply provides a little more direction towards what you all desire.

With your theme in mind, you will have a much easier time with your planning, especially if you choose a planned trip and go more into depth with activities and lodging, etc. If you don't have anything to orient your plans around, and don't know what general experience you even want, it's like a ship leaving port and just floating aimlessly. Of course you'll still have experiences, but you will probably miss the paradise of an island a mile off your course because you didn't do the brief research to know it existed, just one beautiful bridge away. If you named your trip, "Tropical

Adventure," that could encompass everything tropical and you would have discovered the island in your planning and made an effort to explore it.

The point is, a theme makes you think of opportunities to experience things you generally wouldn't; it forces you to think outside the box while giving some insight. You may not have thought to bring s'mores and hot chocolate for your camping adventure, but you remembered because you made the trip a camping theme!

DESTINATION-BASED ROADTRIP THEME

When you are driving your route which was planned around a theme, you can anticipate what is ahead with excitement and curiosity. If your trip is defined by a particular event and destination, you can research the various routes available and give a theme to your travel to and from or even call it the name of the event to make it more fun.

For example, I have an upcoming **destination-based** trip for my friends Brandon and Aimee's wedding and I will definitely make a roadtrip out of it. I will call this: "Brandon and Aimee's Wedding Roadtrip," or even "Epic Boston Roadtrip." With 1,400 miles to cover, there will be plenty of opportunities for adventures. The overall theme will be one of celebration, adventure, and experiencing each area of the eastern US in all of its glory, from southern food in Georgia to checking out the history of aviation in North Carolina, visiting the Capitol in Washington, DC, and then wedding festivities and lots of lobster!

Never, ever, *just* drive.

>   Long car travel should always be
>   turned into memorable experiences.

Theme alters how you will plan your route (you have a general purpose and are seeking adventure!) which changes how you'll experience and enjoy the journey.

Determining Theme

ASK YOURSELF, "WHAT DO I WANT?"

Planning a roadtrip is all about getting in touch with your interests, desires, and what experiences you most want to have. A roadtrip turns wishful thinking into real and unforgettable experiences! Here are a few examples you may even recognize:

- I simply want to explore the area around me and enjoy what it has to offer. Call it your "Local Exploration." And then you have clarity to research everything.

- I *want* to go with friends and see snow, go skiing together, hike to a frozen waterfall, stay in a cottage, and have hot chocolate by a fireplace. → "Epic Winter Roadtrip" or "Winter Wonderland"

- I *want* to take a trip with my significant other to somewhere with a totally tropical feel. I want to take a nap in a hammock, enjoy a sunset walk on the beach, and sip piña coladas. I want to learn how to play a Ukulele. → "Tropical Escape Roadtrip"

- I *want* my brother and me to spend some quality time together. I'd love for us to escape to the mountains over the summer, stay in a log cabin, go fishing, and explore winding mountain roads just to see where they lead. → "Bro Adventure Roadtrip"

From these examples, you can see the process: Think of what you want, choose a theme, then name and add details to your roadtrip! There's nothing more official than giving a title to your adventure, and its name also allows you to remember and refer back to it easily: "Hey babe, let's take another Tropical Escape trip this year!"

"Man cannot discover new oceans unless he has the courage to lose sight of the shore."

—Andre Gide

Chapter 8

CHARTS AND MAPS

Regions simplified, using the distance chart and a map for planning

Joshua Tree State Park, California

Now you know that there are three trip types and you can choose to plan these to be more spontaneous or more detailed as either planned or unplanned trips. You also understand giving them a theme by naming them based off of what you want out of the trip, which gives final direction and brings it all together.

From here, you need to understand ranges before we get to the base steps. Because the base steps will refer back to these resources, it's important to set the stage to understand them now.

If your trip is destination-based, using an online map will help you understand the general ranges, 500 miles at a time, which allows you to see where you should stop roughly every evening of your trip on the way to your final destination.

If your trip is experience-based, using those resources will allow you to see how far you can travel within the time frame you have, which will show you what you can experience and what experiences to seek. For example: I live in Florida and have two days—I cannot have a "Winter Wonderland" experience within two days.

In travel-based trips, they will allow you to plan general stopping points each day or so, however you choose to plan your trip.

I have developed the very best guidelines for planning a trip based on how much time you have and a recommended driving range. For a destination-based trip, you already know your destination and can simply break up the trip in sections, driving up to eight hours in a day or up to 500 miles (whatever comes first) and stopping for the evening in whichever region that it places you. Or you can plan to end up in certain key places for the evening by simply driving a little less or leaving a little earlier and driving slightly more; however, try to stick with the guidelines.

An example of this planning within a destination-based trip would be the following: You have from Thursday up to the following Wednesday, which is when you have to be back at work. This provides a total of six travel days. You live in Tampa, Florida and have a friend's bachelor party in Nashville, TN. You would follow the steps listed in planning by beginning with how long you have for this trip and then breaking up the trip in increments of generally eight hours, planning to leave for each evening destination around the same time each morning. I recommend leaving no later than 10am because this would allow you to be at your evening destination by 6pm and still have the evening to enjoy, while giving you plenty of time to enjoy the journey for the day.

Taking this trip, Tampa to Nashville, is approximately 705 miles with an estimated drive time of 9 hours and 44 minutes. Breaking this up into increments would naturally make it a two-day trip up, unless you are limited by time in which case you could make a rare exception and do it in one day. (However, by doing that you won't fully be able to maximize the journey, which is why the recommended maximum is eight hours a day to allow you to take your time up and enjoy an evening at the destination.) Getting back to the planning, taking that 705 mile trip, you can break it up however you like. Here are two examples:

OPTION A—A SLIGHTLY QUICKER ROUTE

Leave Tampa by 6am on Thursday morning and head to Atlanta 455 miles away, or approximately 6 hours and 45 minutes. Arriving by 1pm (don't forget to stop briefly to stretch your legs every two hours to stay fresh and switch drivers, if possible) and stopping for an hour for lunch in Atlanta before heading to Nashville 250 miles away, or 4 hours—arriving before 6:30pm at your main destination of Nashville and having all evening Thursday. This option would allow you all day Friday, Saturday, Sunday and Monday before heading back Tuesday morning to follow the same route back, arriving home Tuesday evening.

OPTION B—FOCUSING MORE ON THE JOURNEY

Alright, let's say it's a friend's bachelor or bachelorette party in Nashville, but it's one of those friends who you love but can only tolerate in doses. Since you don't want to spend three days with them, yet want to show your support, you decide you want more of an experienced-based trip with your final destination being Nashville. So this technically is a destination-based trip, but you're tweaking it more into an experienced-based trip since you are more focused on the experiences with a plan to swing by the party. You may even have a friend in Atlanta or Savannah, and want to take your time on the way up to visit briefly with them. Here's the route for you:

Leaving Tampa by 7am on Thursday morning and heading to Ginnie Springs as stop one (beautiful natural springs 2 hours and 27 minutes away), arriving by 11am. Here you can stretch your legs and enjoy the crystal clear water of northern Florida for a couple of hours before heading to your next destination of Savannah, Georgia, where you arrive before 5pm. This includes stopping anytime you like to see views, stretch your legs every couple of hours, etc. You would have all Thursday evening in Savannah to enjoy and can spend the night. Friday morning you could leave by 8am and arrive in Atlanta by 1pm for lunch for an hour or so and then head to your ultimate destination of Nashville, arriving before 6:30pm or earlier for the bachelor party that evening! You would have all day Sunday and leave Monday morning by 7am to head back.

Generally aiming to take a different route on the way back, you can plan to stop back in Atlanta, which is four hours away, arriving by 12pm and having lunch before heading to Gainesville, Florida for the evening, arriving by 6:30pm. Tuesday morning leave by 10am and arrive back In Tampa by 1pm with plenty of time to relax and reflect on your roadtrip before heading back to work on Wednesday.

You may question, why not just drive another two to three hours and get home late? This is ultimately up to you and your preferences; however, it truly affects more than you think. In my experience, this is truly not worth it because the time you save will typically be spent sleeping as it will wear you out while taking away from your experiences during the trip back. By going to bed around the same time each evening and waking up at about the same general time each morning, and driving no more than eight hours while taking quick pit stops every two hours, you say fresh. You literally could sustain this every day and not get worn out.

However, when you try to overextend yourself and push for those extra hours and distance, it not only throws you off, but it naturally makes you more destination-based which takes away from the trip and creates a false sense of urgency. This will stress you out and you won't have the desire to stop and enjoy the journey while draining you. It's a fine line, driving just enough to make distance but still enjoying the driving and the

Chapter 8: Charts and maps

experiences you encounter along the way. When you overextend yourself, it not only throws of your sleep cycle and entire body, but also will cause you to potentially have negative feelings associated with roadtrips.

In conclusion, you can modify anything to your wants and needs; however, always try to stick to the roadtrip commandments and other guidelines while using maps and charts as great reference points, while also using a website like MapQuest to put everything into perspective.

Maps help you see the general daily driving ranges so you can have an idea of where you must stop each evening before continuing your trip the next day.

Try to get a quantified idea of how far you can travel, while still enjoying a relaxed roadtrip, based off how much time you have available for the particular trip.

USING THESE RESOURCES FOR EXPERIENCED-BASED TRIPS:

Follow the roadtrip planning steps and start with how much time you have. In this instance, you have determined that this trip is an experience-based trip which means there is no set destination; rather, you simply want to take a roadtrip for experiences. What do you want to experience and where can you go to experience these things? Based off of how long you have, where are you capable of traveling to, while still keeping the correct drive-to-stay ratios of time on the road vs. time at a destination. Your final destination should be your turning point (the place you stay the longest and do not proceed any further away from home; your furthest stop). You always want to allow for at least one day to relax and take a break from driving to enjoy the final destination before returning home; therefore, your max distance is going to be how far you can get in eight hours in each consecutive day while taking into consideration having more time at your destination than time spent driving.

Of course you can adjust the plan so you can drive more the first day in order to reach the destination, then spend less time at the chosen destination and take a different route home; however, these are simply guidelines as it's necessary that you get a break before heading home.

For simplicity let's say there's 12 hours in a "day." As we previously discussed, driving at night is not recommended, and you generally want to spend more time out of the car than in. So, if you're going to spend more than eight hours a day driving to the main destination and eight hours on the way back, make sure you give yourself at least a full day in between to enjoy.

IT'S ALL ABOUT THE RATIOS

Don't be awake more than 16 hours! Strive to have a 1:1 ratio of sleep vs. drive minimum (example for a day trip: four hours driving to destination, eight hours there and four hours back would be a 1:1 ratio) to stay fresh and not get rundown by your trip. Yes it is possible to drive across the country and be refreshed when you arrive if you follow the commandments and stop appropriately.

DISTANCE CHART

1 day vacay = Up to four hours of driving each way (250 mile range)

Allow a max of four hours driving to destination, which means eight hours total drive time, and eight hours to enjoy; 1:1 ratio. So you have one day and can drive to any destination within four hours away, then you have all day to enjoy before driving the four hours home.

Example: 6am–10am driving / 10am–6pm enjoy / 6pm -10pm driving back. So if you have only one day, you can follow the ratios and maps to plan an enjoyable day trip.

2 days vacay = (Up to 250-500 miles each way)

Allow a max of eight hours driving each way, which allows you 24 hours to enjoy. Example: Leave 6am Friday and drive until 2pm. Have all afternoon and evening (from 2pm on), as well as the next morning and mid-day. Leave by 2pm Saturday for the return trip and arrive Saturday night.

3 days vacay = Up to one day of travel each way (500 miles or slightly more)

Allow a max of eight hours to drive to your destination since this does not increase anymore according to the commandments, but this simply increases your leisure time which allows you 36 hours at your destination. Use a map to get an idea of different ranges near you and also what is around your general region.

Any distances after would allow you to slowly extend your driving range.

4 days vacay = One and a half days travel each way (Up to 750 miles each way)

Allow a max of eight hours to your nightly destination, so the first day you could get up to eight hours (500 miles) away; day two maybe another four hours (250 miles), extending your range while still allowing you to enjoy a day and a half at your destination.

5 days vacay = Two days travel each way (up to 1,000 miles each way)

Allow a max of eight hours to your nightly destination, so the first day you could get up to eight hours (500 miles) away. Day two could be up to 500 miles as well, which would have you arriving at your destination by 6pm on the second day, leaving you the evening in addition to a full day and then all morning until about 10am to head back the same distance.

6 days vacay = Two days travel each way or slightly more (up to 1,250 miles each way)

Allow a max of eight hours to your nightly destination, so the first day you could get up to eight hours (500 miles) away); your second day up to 500 miles and then have an evening, two solid days and a morning to relax before heading back.

"Remember that happiness is a way of travel, not a destination."

–*Roy M. Goodman*

Chapter 9

CREATING THE FOUNDATION

Part 1 of simplifying the planning process, steps 1-3

Building our first igloo on Mammoth Mountain, CA

THE FIRST GENERAL BASE STEPS

1. **SET YOUR FOUNDATION (Time Parameters)**

    - How long do you have for this trip?

    - What is the earliest you can leave (day/time)?

    - What is the latest you can be back home (day/time)?

    - Plan on leaving and arriving at those times, but make it early and late enough to allow flexibility because chances are it will run an hour late, so add some time in the beginning and end of trip.

Overview: Decide when you need to leave and return, so you can determine the destination and turning point, and route details. For example: I have three days, so I can leave Friday morning at 8am but need to be back Sunday night by 8pm. Once you have the beginning and ending noted, you have a **Time Frame** to work with for all other plans.

2. **DESTINATION-BASED TRIP, EXPERIENCE-BASED OR TRAVEL-BASED?**

The trip will always be one of three types: **Destination-based**, which would be a roadtrip with plans based on an event or reason to be in a certain place by a set time. For example, I am going to attend a wedding in Boston and planning a roadtrip for the journey. This trip type is slightly more destination-focused and will emphasize getting to your destination quicker while still taking time to enjoy the journey, and may take the same route up as it does back home. Or, it will be **experience-based**, where you plan to take a roadtrip and enjoy what each surrounding area has to offer, along with seeking certain key experiences, though you may still choose a final destination where you spend the most time. This final destination would be where you seek to experience the majority of what you desire. Taking your time on the way up and enjoying everything along the way, you'd then head home on a different route at a slow pace.

Planning to seek these experiences is often dependent on where you are and where you can travel comfortably within your distance range. (Refer to the recommended roadtrip ranges previously shown based on your general time frame.)

Lastly, your trip might be **travel-based,** which is simply a trip with continuous movement where you do not have any set final destination. Each stop at a destination is for generally the same period of time before proceeding to the next in a giant loop from the time you leave home back around to it. This would be simply stopping in a different city each day or even more, making sure to stay within the 500-mile driving limit per day to stay fresh and enjoy each daily journey.

So, ask yourself:

- Do I need to be at a specific place at a certain day and time for an event such as a friend's wedding, concert, road race, or other event? If so, my trip type is **destination-based**. I will enjoy the journey up and plan accordingly, though I'll generally try to get to my destination as fast as possible within the guidelines and will plan to spend the majority of my time there.

- Do I simply want to take a roadtrip that allows me to experience as many things as possible on my way to and home from a final destination? If so, my trip type is **experience-based**. I want to take a trip with friends and just explore the countryside and go camping somewhere, or I want to go skiing and enjoy everything associated with winter up north, from hot chocolate to cozy fire places and building a snowman. For this you would use the guidelines and ultimately choose a destination for these experiences based on how long you have and how far you can travel to an area that offers these experiences, and then break the trip up into sections and take your time enjoying the trip up, trying to maximize the journey by then taking a different route home.

My trip is **travel-based** if I want to take off, generally without any set destinations, and generally no idea of any key experiences that I want, aside from exploration. I have 10 days and just want to get away. I have always wanted to experience certain cities, such as St. Augustine, Savannah, Helen, Ashville, etc. and I'll plan a long trip that loops them all for about the same time in each.

3.   **ESTABLISH A THEME! (What You Want to Experience)**

Choosing a theme allows you to appreciate your adventure more by immersing yourself further in it. To give a context and provide a framework for the many decisions to make before and during your trip, you need to choose a **theme**. Knowing your theme will help you find and accomplish more of the key experiences you want. Of course your roadtrip will provide many spur-of-the-moment opportunities and you want to take advantage of what comes along, but you can ensure that you will experience more of what you want through some planning around your theme. Simply put, it will give you more direction while helping you appreciate the trip more. You can define your theme by considering any of the following:

Theme Ideas

- What the surrounding areas have to offer
- Event or events to experience
- Different seasons to enjoy
- Activities
- History
- Key attractions

Make a list of the experiences you most want! This list helps provide the framework for your research later. I suggest making it fun and naming your trip once you determine your theme. For example, I will be driving from Florida to Tennessee in late October, an ideal time for a fall-themed roadtrip. My plans will include seeing beautiful fall foliage, Halloween festivals, and pumpkin spice-flavored everything! Name of trip: "Fall Adventure Roadtrip."

Use the Theme Ideas list for some helpful prompts, keeping in mind that having a theme is simply to make your roadtrip richer in memorable experiences. Rather than driving aimlessly or only focusing on getting to the destination, a theme is a great way to enhance your trip.

BRINGING IT TOGETHER-PART 1

If you've followed along, you now know your **time frame**, which is how many days and hours you have to work with as you begin planning. You have an idea of how far you can travel and how long you can stay. And you have determined if your trip is **destination-based**, **experienced-based**, or **travel-based**. You've chosen your **theme**, and your roadtrip even has a **name**! You now have the structure and a good idea of what you want to experience. With these in place, you are beginning to have the foundation needed for your epic trip.

"The gladdest moment in human life, I think, is a departure into unknown lands."

– Sir Richard Burton

Chapter 10

BUILDING AN EPIC TRIP

Part 2 of simplifying the planning process, steps 4-6

4. SET REGIONS

USING THE MAPS, DETERMINE AN AREA FOR EACH OF YOUR REFERENCE POINTS.

Take the total distance of your trip and divide it into 500-mile increments, which equates to about eight hours of driving time per stretch. Try to pick major cities for now, as this will give you a framework to work within. These will be the cities that you choose to sleep in each evening and will be called reference points. I'll show you how and why you may want to tweak this as your plans progress.

Based on eight-hour driving stretches along your journey, these reference points can vary—for example, if you want to stay later in the day in the city where you spent the previous night instead of leaving by 2pm, that is fine, but you will still need to follow the Commandments and stop at your next layover by 6:30pm. This means the next base will be closer than 500 miles, which is a choice that may work best for you to be able to enjoy your experiences. You always want to feel like you have flexibility and choices at hand, but for the best roadtrip overall, do stay within the bounds of the Commandments.

If you don't reach your base by 6:30 in the evening and just keep driving, you will fall behind on your drive recovery time. You'll end up going to bed later and sleeping in later, and the cumulative effect is exhausting. It's so important, I'll state it again: Only drive eight hours a day or less, during the daylight, and arrive at your destination for that evening by 6:30pm at the latest! There is no set number of stops in between your bases, but keep your eye on the time you spend while on breaks (which you should take every two hours). If you are not yet nearing your planned base stop by 6pm, you'll need to look for an alternate place to stop by 6:30pm. (Refer back to the Technology section earlier for app suggestions to help find last-minute hotel deals, etc.)

Each city you initially choose as a stop can change to another one in the general region, but by identifying a larger-sized city within the eight-hour driving guidelines, you will have a good reference point. Then you can do an online search to see what is of interest to you in that area. You can modify your planned route to be slightly east or slightly north, for example.

A great example is when my friend said the highlight of her roadtrip with her daughter was staying at a lodge near the top of Mount Rainier. Their destination-based trip took them to Seattle, but at the last moment she realized she did not have to stay in a mediocre hotel in town because Mount Rainier was a relatively short drive out of the city and the room at the lodge on the side of the gorgeous 14,000 ft. mountain was the same price.

Take your trip, break it down into 500-mile increments and choose reference points, then you can research the surrounding region of each reference point to either change the nightly destination or add stops between on the way to each one to enjoy the journey.

5. Possible Destination and Routes

For all types of trips, use an online map of America—for an interactive one, simply open mapquest.com. If it's a destination-based trip, it will help you determine an idea of how far to drive each day and what areas you can potentially pass through. If it's an experience-based trip, you'll see how far you can travel based on your time frame, and thus discover your destination options, as well as if it's travel-based.

This ensures you don't have to rush and cram a lot of the return driving in on one day. You don't want to cut it so close you risk being back late for an appointment or work. The distance map makes it easy to see what your potential final destinations can be, based on your time frame, which provides the framework for planning.

Take that framework and now go deeper, based off of your theme and what you want to experience. Ask yourself these questions, and let Google or any online searching reveal the best attractions, must-dos, and unique features of each region.

Research Questions

- Based on your theme, what key experiences do you want?
- What regions are you passing through and what does each have to offer?
- What key cities are within your final destination range?
- What key cities offer experiences that fit with your theme?
- Are there any smaller cities or attractions?
- What does the surrounding area have to offer each day along your route?

This is easy if your trip is destination-based because you will simply be choosing between various routes to get to your destination and back (and bases along the way). If your trip is experience-based, then building off the last question, this will be defined as either the furthest point at which you drive before heading back, or the destination that offers the most of what you want to experience and where you'll spend most of your time.

Stay tuned for the next book of this series which will provide actual detailed, **themed routes** to help with planning: *Choose Your Dream Adventure.*

6. Research Time—Work Backwards

USING GOOGLE AND MAPQUEST

Use MapQuest as a guide opened on one webpage, which allows you to put the city you're leaving from and your final destination and see the general route.

I always open MapQuest on one page, and Google on another, and have a notepad out as I plan. You can create a totally customized trip plan. If you want, it is then easy to share the trip via text or email to yourself and others.

Always try to take a different way home than the route you took heading out, if possible, by utilizing the map page showing the route (or route options).

A couple of Google searches can be all you need and this can be a very enjoyable part of the planning process. Review the previous steps and review it all after some final research.

- Your ultimate destination city (whether it is experienced-based, destination-based or travel-based)
- Your theme, what experiences you want to search for, and in which areas/cities to find them
- Your framework, with an idea of what general area you need to stop every eight hours for the evening

You can then either change that destination for the evening to another city in the surrounding area, or build on it with attractions you found.

With MapQuest open you can have another browser open for research on each city and plug in each potential hotspot along the general route to insure it is not too far out of the way, for example, and then work your way down to where you are.

Chapter 10: Building an epic trip

You can research must-sees in the area along those guidelines which allows you to determine the possible routes. You did your research based on your overall theme, which helps you choose locations, while you also enjoy locations for what they offer.

If your trip is destination-based, you can research the key cities and attractions for a possible route there and a different route back, along with theme-related attractions that are revealed as you look at what the surrounding area offers.

Each of these steps is designed to bring you closer and closer to having the best plan possible for your epic roadtrip adventure, so let's go!

> ***"Travel brings power and love back into your life."***
>
> —*Rumi*

Chapter 11

PREPARING

Part 3 of simplifying the planning process, parts 7-8

Finding a snowman in a forest in Mammoth Lakes mid-December

Continuing on with the final 2 steps

6. What is my weather forecast? What activities will I be doing?

There is an art and science to packing. You want to take only what you need, yet everything you need. Check the weather forecasted along your route and what activities you will be doing throughout the trip. Choose clothes, shoes, and gear to match the potential temperatures and wet/dry conditions. Also consider your theme and activities: If you plan to hike, bring hiking gear! (See upcoming tips on packing—it's simpler than you think!)

7. Do I want a planned trip or unplanned?

If this will be one of your *planned* roadtrips, you will have more research, decisions, and details to handle pre-trip. You need to map your route and choose each stopover city. Book your lodging in advance and use the internet to check out the restaurants, other travelers' recommendations, and attractions in each area. Maybe you need to make a reservation in advance with an outfitter for that kayak adventure. Take your planning to any level your heart desires, but leave timeframes general to avoid stress.

If you want more of an *unplanned* trip, you now have enough information to simply use the packing list and take off. Good luck and have a great trip!! You can use technology to find a place to stay last minute and help with other last minute decisions! When you get to an area you feel like exploring, the internet can reveal all kinds of activities and sights to see nearby, yet many off the beaten path.

I definitely recommend getting the experience of both types of trips under your belt. Sometimes it's nice to have everything already thought out and know where you'll be stopping to sleep so you can just relax. It's equally nice to take an adventurous roadtrip, and play it by ear within the guidelines. It just depends on what you feel when it gets closer to your trip.

If its intent is to be more of a relaxing getaway to get a break from work and recover after a long few weeks, you may be more interested in a planned trip—you may not have the extra energy and patience for the unknown.

Chapter 11: Preparing

Conversely, if you are tired of routines, agendas, and responsibilities and are taking a trip to escape and have the adventure of a lifetime—then an unplanned roadtrip could be perfect! It is all about timing and what's best for you for this particular trip. Go with what you are attracted to and interested in—both planned and unplanned trips can turn out great, trust me.

BRINGING IT ALL TOGETHER

You now understand the dynamics of trip types, themes, and how to use the distance recommendations and a map in planning. Let's look at an example for each trip type, beginning with a destination-based trip.

ROAD TRIPPIN THE RIGHT WAY
A COMPLETE EXAMPLE: A PLAN IS BORN

My name is Jonathan and I currently live in Sarasota, Florida and I have a friend's wedding in Charlotte, NC on August 16th.

I will begin with the first three base steps:

- **How long do I have for this trip?**
- **What is the earliest (day/time) I can leave?**
- **What is the latest (day/time) I can return?**

I have one week, 7 days total for the trip. I can leave Wednesday morning at 6am on the 14th of August and need to be back Tuesday the 20th, by 7pm, so I can unpack and get to sleep early before work the next day. I'll plan on leaving by 6am, but I will have my trip planned out as if I left at 7am, because chances are things will run late as I try to leave in the morning. I'll also plan to get home by 6pm on that Tuesday in case things run later that last day on the trip home. This gives me a nice framework, the parameters are set!

- **Is this trip destination-based or theme-based?**

The trip is destination-based and I have to be there by that Thursday the 15th so I can be ready for the wedding the next day.

- **What is my theme?**

I just want to experience the open road and anything that comes my way along this trip, nothing specific, just what each region along the way offers. I'll call it "Epic Wedding Roadtrip" and will seek to just meet people and have as much fun as possible along the way. Actually, it is fall and there will be beautiful fall colors along the way—I'll change it to: "Epic Fall Wedding Roadtrip." Now it will guide me to experience the autumn foliage beauty, along with everything else.

SETTING REGIONS, WALK THROUGH EXAMPLE

I opened MapQuest on one page and Google on another and I have a notepad to take notes.

Entering my home city and my destination, it now shows me a route that is 11 hours and 26 minutes long and even shows me estimated fuel cost.

Taking this route, I use the maps and MapQuest to divide it up into a route with stops every eight hours, or 500 miles, as a framework to work from. By clicking to choose "add stop," I can input the nearest major city along the route within each 500 mile range, one at a time, check each distance. The destination may need to be adjusted to keep the driving plan within the guidelines. -I realize that adjusting to visit key cities may add an hour or two for the total trip, but this is completely worth it since it's about the journey and I have the time!

- *I can then do some research on each city and decide if i want to keep those cities as my destination for each evening or choose somewhere a little off the route for different attractions that I find. I can adjust these base points accordingly.*

- *I now have my framework complete and can have fun googling any key places between cities to check out throughout the journey and add these to my plan.*

- *I now have a pretty good idea about where im going and what im doing, so what am i going to pack to be ready for the weather and activities?*

Chapter 11: Preparing

- Lastly, do i want a planned trip or unplanned trip? If I decide on a planned trip, I will book hotels in advance in these destination and potentially even reserve my place in certain activities and even dinner reservations. For this time I decide on an unplanned trip, so im literally going to just pack and take off, wing it and find a hotel in each base city for the night and then play it by ear on activities and exploring.

As for the exact route, I decided to plan my stops as follows:

1st stop–*St. Augustine, Florida,* which is 3 hours and 43 minutes away (236 miles). Of course I will stop briefly (two hours in) to stretch my legs, but St. Augustine will be my first place to explore. This is not where I will spend the night, so I will enjoy the city and leave after 3 hours and head to my next stop. The time breakdown would be the following: Leaving by 6am on Wednesday the 14th, planning on the additional hour, I would arrive in St. Augustine no later than 11am. I'll have lunch and explore a little, and leave by 2pm.

2nd stop- *Savannah, Georgia,* which is a 2 hour and 44 minute drive from St. Augustine (176 miles). I will stop 2 hours in to stretch my legs, wherever that is and continue on. Savannah will then be my stop to sleep since it is close to where an eight-hour drive would take me on this first day. I would rather not try to drive another hour or so to sleep in some random small city when Savannah is such a hotspot and has the most to offer in the area. I should arrive in Savannah by 5pm, but because I'm adding the additional 1.5 hours potential drive time to every 4 hours scheduled (to prevent stress and allow me time to explore along the journey), I will plan on arriving by 6:30pm at the latest. I will have ample time to stop at local peach stands and maybe at a nice park to take a quick walk when I am 2 hours in. I'll arrive right on time (or early) and get a hotel. I can then enjoy seeing Savannah and all the key attractions for the evening as well as the following morning and lunchtime. I will leave by 2pm the next day.

3rd stop- *My destination of* **Charlotte, North Carolina,** *is only 3 hours and 54 minutes away (252 miles). I will arrive here well before 6:30 pm! I can enjoy the entire evening here, go out with friends, and get ready for the wedding the following day.*

HEADING HOME

After great times Friday and Saturday, I will plan to leave Sunday morning. To head back to Sarasota, I want to take a different route to get some other experiences along the way home.

1st stop- *Leave Sunday by 7am and head to* **Charleston, South Carolina,** *3 hours and 17 min away (210 miles). After driving 2 hours, I will take a break. I'll arrive in Charleston by 11am and check out this historic city and have some true southern food and leave by 12:30pm.*

2nd stop- *Gainesville, Florida, which is 5 hours and 6 min away (306 miles). Of course I'll stop every two hours to stretch my legs and enjoy the scenery, maybe a snack. I will arrive by 6:30pm and check into a hotel. I'll drive or walk around to see the University of Florida campus and have dinner, then get to bed.*

3rd stop- *Orlando, Florida, one hour and 47 min away (112 miles). Monday morning I will leave by 7am, take a break after two hours, and arrive in Orlando by 10am. I don't have time to visit major attractions, but I'll have a nice breakfast and explore downtown Orlando, walk around Lake Eola, and see what the locals (vs. tourists) are up to. I can take up to 3 hours if i choose, but I should head out by 1pm.*

Last stop, *home sweet home! I'll arrive back in Sarasota 2 hours and 6 min later (132 miles) by 3:30 pm–ahead of schedule!*

Summary: *I got to experience six different cities for the first time and every key experience within each one that I haven't mentioned. I never drove more than two hours at a time, and there was always five hours or less between main attractions. I got to enjoy the trip up to the wedding destination city, and then both Friday and Saturday there. I had an interesting trip back on a different route. There was something to look forward to the entire trip!*

Chapter 11: Preparing

"Twenty years from now you will be more disappointed by the things you didn't do than by the ones you did do."

– Mark Twain

Chapter 12

THE NITTY GRITTY

Essentials, packing list, taking advantage of technology, associated costs and safety

Parking Garage in Del Mar, California about to start the cross country trip back to Florida

THE PACKING PROCESS SIMPLIFIED

Once you learn the secrets, you will have a change of heart about packing. Instead of dreading it, you'll think it's easy. I'm going to make this process as simple as possible.

If you travel a lot, or want to begin traveling often and seamlessly, this system will make everything very efficient. At the same time, this structure may frighten some, so take it as a guideline—or for my fellow OCD types, follow it as an exact guide. The more preparation you do in advance, the easier the packing process can be. It can literally be made to take no more than 10 minutes.

If you don't travel often, use these lists to ensure you have everything you need, while if you do travel often, you'll want to put together four small bags/kits that you can simply grab and go for efficiency. Imagine having a personal hygiene bag that has all your bathroom essentials, a travel kit that has anything you may need while on the road, an emergency roadside kit that you can throw in your trunk and feel safe, and lastly a cooler for your food storage and utensils. If you had these kits prepped in advance, you could simply throw them inside your car, pack and be out the door within 15 minutes without anything to worry about. Though your bathroom kit can be packed in your main bag with clothes, it must be easily accessible. What if you want to brush your teeth while on the road or wash your face somewhere? You don't want to have to dig through everything; it's all about convenience and efficiency.

1. **A personal care hygiene** kit that you can just grab and pack. It should contain a set of each item and product you use, separate from the containers in your bathroom. By setting up a new bathroom kit rather than taking what you already have in your restroom, it's easier to pack and unpack. When you leave, you grab your travel hygiene kit, and when you return you throw it in its place in the closet. Packing and unpacking becomes seamless. It's okay to use small, travel-sized products, and just replace them when they get low. Trust me, this is worth taking the time to set up! It provides so much convenience rather than leaving everything out to use up until the last minute and then trying to throw all your bathroom essentials in a bag and usually forgetting toothpaste or

your face wash and when you return you don't have to take out all those little items again.

2. **Car travel kit:** An accessory travel bag to keep in the car with you for the duration of the roadtrip. Pack what you want handy: sunscreen, hand sanitizer, lip balm, tissues, a notepad and pens (very useful when writing down thoughts, researching places in the area, things you find as reminders, etc.), hat, mobile phone charger, sunglasses (drastically reduces eye fatigue and prevents pinguecula), lightweight rain poncho, water bottle, bandage strips (in case of blisters). You can also keep your wallet or ID here if you are short on pockets, but you'll need to keep it extra safe from theft. These items are often overlooked, but trust me—each one has a distinct purpose!

   This bag could simply a little drawstring bag or hiking backpack, whatever your style is for day excursions to have something to put your items in when exploring, while having key things you may need while in the car. This will be your active-use bag to grab and take when you leave the car or hotel room. Chances are you'll be doing a lot of walking and exploring, whether hiking up a path in Virginia or walking along the sidewalks from site to site in Washington, DC. You need a bag for essentials that you may need while away from home base.

   Personally, I like a small backpack for hiking or walking around a city because it leaves my hands free and is also less apt to be set down and accidentally left behind. The web site for Camel Pak has a variety of day packs to choose from, even waist packs, roll-tops, and hydration packs. Just think about your own needs and size—kid-sized packs are available, too; however, one per car should be sufficient for everyone, unless you'll be splitting up and doing separate activities often.

3. **Emergency roadside kit** in the trunk: Have a Roadtrip Emergency Auto Tool (which includes a glass breaker) should be kept handy, and a flashlight and a small folding knife in your console, as these three come in handy. While A full emergency kit can be left in your trunk and can include various items such as a first aid kit, etc.

(Refer to the list below for some more ideas.) An example of the importance of having the 3 items in your car- imagine you don't follow the road trip commandments and find yourself driving at night and you get a flat tire in the middle of a heavily wooded area. If you want to change your tire you need a flashlight handy or you'll have very limited visibility and who wants to be digging through their trunk looking for their only flashlight , in the middle of a forest at night in the dark! The knife is useful to have within to cut packages if you purchase things or even fruit, etc... while the emergency auto tool ensures an easy escape from your vehicle if ever needed. If the vehicle is yours, I would simply leave the knife, flashlight and auto emergency tool in the center console or glove box all year around because they are always useful items.

4. **A cooler**, preferably one with pockets, and you can get reusable silverware—a great option is a reusable fork, spoon and knife tool that comes in a kit with a stainless steel straw and brush, available for purchase at sustainablebreakthroughs.com—so you can protect the environment. Don't forget a roll of paper towels, some hand towelettes, a couple small plastic bags, and a couple of trash bags. Try to find a cooler that allows you to store these items in different pockets to keep everything food related together; however, any cooler and a bag will work to store your food and these items.

Imagine how seamless the packing and traveling process would be with a little planning in advance. If you had each one of these small bags set up once and stored them in a garage or closet and, when it came time for a trip, you simply threw them in your car along with your travel bag and took off, you could relax in knowing that you have everything you need!

Example (because I like to paint the picture): I decide to take a 3 day weekend trip from Florida to North Carolina for a camping trip. I grab my Emergency roadside kit and throw it in the car trunk in the back. I grab my cooler, pack it with food and throw it in my backseat. I grab my travel bag with the accessories and throw it in the passenger seat. Lastly I grab my bathroom kit, throw it in my clothes bag, along with whatever clothes I packed and throw it in the trunk. I take off and head out!

Chapter 12: The nitty gritty

Without pre-packing any of these things, getting ready to leave is a long packing process. Of course you don't have to listen and you can skip out on the cooler, or car travel bag, or emergency roadside kit, but you're setting yourself up for disaster...trust me! You will always have anything you need and packing will be simple if you listen.

LUGGAGE

Factoring into your choice for luggage are personal preference, length of your trip, theme and activities to plan for, and room in your vehicle (affected by size of car and number of travelers). Your choice of baggage could be anything from a large backpack or a duffle bag to larger suitcases.

Generally, **two bags** are what I recommend:

- One large travel bag for all clothes and wearables EXCEPT shoes and coats. Include your personal hygiene kit and a large trash bag or laundry bag to collect dirty clothes throughout the trip.

- A medium-sized bag for all shoes, with a couple plastic grocery bags in a side pocket to use to wrap dirty shoes post-hiking before putting them back in the main bag (or keep separate if there is room).

ESSENTIALS/ PACKING
How to dress, what to pack in your car and travel bag

51% of vacationers said they would rather give up alcohol for a month and social media for a week, than have to pack, according to one study. Packing can seem overwhelming as there are so many different categories and situations to pack for. In addition to deciding on all the contents to bring along, you have to figure out where everything can be placed.

Let's take the struggle out of packing right now! For simplicity and ease, simply follow these steps:

1. Use the base steps and plan your trip. You will need to know, for example, your trip theme and associated weather and activities in order to know what to bring.

2. Clear a large area on your bed or clean floor, as you will cover it with piles (one pile for each day of your trip plus a few other categories). Start with clothes, particularly underwear and socks, and then work your way to outer layers. For each day of your trip, pack two pairs of underwear and socks, giving you the option to change for an evening out. Both men and women should consider different possible activities and bring a mix of regular and sports-wear, and both short socks and high socks (for hiking, etc.). Keep your theme and potential activities in mind as you choose your attire.

3. Begin by laying out two pairs of socks and two undergarments to start each pile which represents each day. Now you have your separate bases to add to.

4. Make one additional pile with your sleepy-time clothes, whatever they may be. If you usually sleep in your birthday suit, then you will save a little space! However, if you don't sleep naked, add your pajamas, two or more, depending on the duration of your trip. Now think workout clothes! Depending on the trip route, your theme, and personal preference, you may want to work out. Add one or two sports outfits and shoes to this pile.

5. Accessories! Make a pile to add a belt, any hats, watches, or small items that you want to bring (so you don't forget them). Think of anything you'll possibly need: a phone charger, GPS, watch or jewelry, water bottles, adventure gear, etc.! Jackets, beanies, gloves, swim suits, and don't forget to add your bathroom kit to this pile but make it easily accessible, packed at the top.

6. Congrats, you're making progress! Now on to the last step. You can play it conservatively, or not, depending on the dynamics of your trip; it's up to you. The framework is there and now you can simply think of what you would wear each day. It's better to have slightly more than to run out of clean clothes, so to play it safe pick

Chapter 12: The nitty gritty

a couple casual outfits, and a couple nicer outfits, a combination of jeans, shorts, t-shirts and nice button down.

It really depends on trip dynamics and what you'll be doing, but generally you want a mix of active wear and nice clothes for day festivities and going out. You could pick one active outfit one per day and one nice outfit one per day but this may be excessive. Again, it just depends on preference, how long your trip is, and how many people are coming—which affects the luggage size you can bring. You can generally wear the same shorts or jeans more than once, to save space.

7. Lastly, what will you wear on your first day of driving? Set this outfit aside and pack the rest. I recommend something very comfortable and preferably shoes that can slide off relatively easily, to rest your feet as a passenger or on breaks.

- You should now have a pile of underwear and socks for each day of the trip

- A pile for sleep wear, workout clothes /active wear

- A pile for accessories

- A pile for your main clothes, consisting of a combination of casual and nice, which you can even take it a step further, if you'd like to, by dividing them up and adding them to the underwear and sock piles you've started for each day to ensure you have the right clothes when needed.

- Also by now you've picked out your clothes for the first drive day and set them aside. The rest are packed and you're ready to go!

Congrats!

HOW TO DRESS

After answering the base questions you will have the knowledge of what clothes to pack. If you don't have much experience riding in a car for long stretches, you may think that to "dress comfortably" means jeans, a t-shirt, and tennis shoes, like you'd wear to be comfortable during a marathon shopping trip at the mall. Sitting is different. I always recommend wearing something comfortable such as sweatpants or basketball shorts, and loose-fitting shoes that you can slip out of relatively easily (but not sandals or flip-flops if you are the driver). Also, bring a light jacket and a light blanket in the car. They both come in handy, especially in the passenger seat when you want to be cozier.

Of course you should pack according to the regions you are going. If you are going on a trip with cold weather and snow, pack all the heavy jackets in the trunk, last (on top), so they are easily accessible. Because cold weather clothes and accessories take up so much space, rather than trying to pack them each individually, your best bet is to put every traveler's cold-weather necessities, such as gloves, hats and scarves, in one large bag. A trash bag works fine unless you have a duffle bag, which would be even better.

PUTTING TOGETHER THE TRAVEL KITS

PERSONAL HYGIENE KIT

Call me crazy, but the convenience of taking 15 minutes and spending $20-$30 maximum, one time, to put together the portable bathroom kit is priceless. It's a pain to try to scavenge around and gather all the miscellaneous bathroom items you need prior to each trip. If you take the time to go to a Walmart or drug store, buy a little portable bathroom bag and fill it up with the following, you will not regret it! Once you do this, you can simply grab it and throw it in a pile along with the rest of your packing and still have your original, everyday bathroom items you need the night and morning before leaving without the risk of forgetting something. The convenience is worth it!

Chapter 12: The nitty gritty

This list is universal, so feel free to adjust it for women or men or individual needs:

- toothbrush
- toothpaste
- comb
- two razors/shaving cream
- small mirror (in case you are camping and need one)
- shampoo/conditioner/body scrub
- hair ties or other hair products
- soap (with zip-lock bag for bar)
- hand sanitizer
- deodorant
- facewash
- feminine products
- lip balm

CAR TRAVEL KIT

This is simply a little bag you bring with you on every roadtrip that has essentials that come in handy on the road.

- hand sanitizer
- sunscreen
- notepad (very useful when writing down thoughts, researching places in an area, things you find as reminders, etc.)
- a couple pens
- mobile phone charger and wall outlet charger
- sunglasses (drastically reduces eye fatigue and prevents pinguecula)
- water bottle
- umbrella
- sun shade car dash cover

COOLER

I prefer a cooler that is inside a slide-on cover that has pockets which helps you stay organized.

- Reusable silverware packs (protect the environment)
- paper towel roll
- backup large trash bag folded up in front pocket
- a couple smaller grocery store bags
- a can opener
- wine key
- a lighter
- bottle opener

EMERGENCY CAR KIT

As I said, The Roadtrip Emergency Auto Tool goes in your car, ideally in the console between the front seats. This one tool features: Strong LED flashlight with switch to strobe setting; built-in magnets to attach the tool (with flashing beacon) to the side or top of your car; automatic punch glass breaker for emergency escape; 110-decibel alarm; and a sharp blade to cut seat-belt for emergency escape. Your additional emergency kit items can travel in your trunk. Suggested items include:

- Jumper cables
- Space blanket
- Flashlight
- Flares
- Triangle reflectors
- Tool kit
- First aid kit
- Quart of motor oil
- Coolant

- Spare tire and tire jack
- Multipurpose tool
- Duct tape

Chances are you'll never use any of these items aside from the jumper cables; however, having a kit with each one of these items gives you peace of mind during potential worst-case scenarios. This would prepare you for breaking down somewhere in the middle of nowhere without cell service. There are usually other drivers, or cell service, etc., so you don't have to worry about this with technology today, but I want to prepare you for anything!

PROVISIONS TO PACK

The last thing you want to have to rely on for snacks is what a gas station may have on hand. Oftentimes, gas stations will be small and have only a very limited selection of any type of real food. Sure, you may find a fruit stand or pull over for "boiled peanuts," but with a little pre-planning you will have a good balance of food and beverages within reach. You want a selection of the following: snack foods, fresh produce, meal options, beverages, and savory sweets. My recommended list will give you a great start to creating your own.

Keep in mind this list is for a long roadtrip, to have everything you would need, so feel free to adjust accordingly:

- A 16-pack of bottled water (with easy access behind the passenger seat), or you can bring reusable bottles for each passenger and just refill them from the main 2.5 gallon water in the trunk.
- 2.5 gallon container with spout (handy for washing hands or cleaning things in the middle of nowhere)
- A couple cans of a caffeinated beverage, just in case you need it
- Tea
- Cold brew coffee
- Juice

- Mixed nuts
- Healthy bars (more protein, less carbs)
- Dark chocolate! (the higher the cocoa content the better, 70%+)
- Healthy version of chips and cookies
- Bananas, apples, tangerines, seedless grapes, or other fruit (this is a must!)
- Peanut butter and honey sandwiches (make at home and pack, they will stay edible for days, even in a hot car, as honey has antibacterial and antifungal properties.
- Turkey sandwiches (if you bring soft tortillas or a loaf of bread and cheese, the possibilities are endless)
- Hummus and crackers or pretzels
- Lots of ice! Unless you buy a thermoelectric cooler that plugs in, such as a Koolatron Voyager.

PACKING PLACEMENT

As I mentioned, I recommend putting the emergency auto tool, knife, and a flashlight in your console, while storing an important documents separately in the glove box or vise versa (so if you get pulled over you don't get yourself in trouble reaching close to a knife to grab papers.) As for the rest, store the emergency roadside kit in the trunk, the personal care kit in your travel bag, which goes in the trunk but remains easily accessible, and keeping the cooler and accessory bag in the car for easy access—the placement of which will depend on the number of travelers.

If it's a full car, then the majority of everything will be in the trunk. If there isn't enough room, consider getting a rooftop carry rack which are available for both vehicles with and without roof racks.

If there are four people or fewer, definitely keep the cooler in the backseat between passengers and the travel kit can be on the floor in the same middle section.

Chapter 12: The nitty gritty

Spending Plan
An estimate on gas and associated expenses, car choice, renting or not, etc.

Gas: At this writing, the national average is $2.66 a gallon, according to AAA. The average miles-per-gallon has been raised to 24 mpg. There are fuel calculators online, but to make it easy, just take your total mileage (round trip) and divide it by your average highway mpg for your vehicle. Then, multiply that by what you pay for gas per gallon (or the national average).

Example: Driving a 2005 Cadillac CTS, gas mileage is about 27 mpg (highway). Driving to Nashville, Tennessee, from Tampa, Florida, is about 704 miles, or a 1,408 mile round trip. Divide this by 27, and that's roughly 52 gallons, times the price of gas of $2.66, equals $138 dollars in gas expense for the entire trip. Not bad!

Lodging: This will often be the bulk of your expenses unless you have other options. All possible options include the following:

- Hotel or motel
- Airbnb
- Camping (bring tent or rent a cabin)
- Friend or relative's place
- Couch surfing
- Sleep in RV if you're pulling one
- Sleep in car (only recommended if you need a nap—not for overnight)

Depending on your budget, you may want to mix it up. If you sleep in your tent one night, stay in a hotel (with a hot shower!) the next, and so on. If you choose to make it a planned trip and book everything in advance, you don't have anything to worry about. If you want to wing it, deciding destinations as you go and finding places to stay last-minute, there are great apps for that such as "Hotel Tonight," which is mentioned in the Technology section. Briefly, it's a free app which provides you a list of hotels in the area that are willing to offer any open rooms at a last-minute discounted rate. You can get great deals this way, but keep in mind that this app does not show *all* hotels in the area, only the ones that were willing to offer the discounted rooms and work with the app. If this app doesn't pan out for you, just use Google to find all the hotel options in your area.

PET FRIENDLY HOTELS

Many hotels will offer dog-friendly rooms, refer back to the end of Chapter 6 for the hotel list. These hotels may charge a ridiculous pet fee that oftentimes can be almost the same price as the room! Because not every hotel allows pets at all, if you have a four-legged traveler, you may want to plan and book your overnight stays ahead of time. But, as long as you are not going too far off the grid on your route, you should be able to find a suitable pet-friendly place. In my travels, La Quinta was always good and never charges pet fees!

SAFETY—BE AWARE OF DANGEROUS VIBRATIONS

Studies at the Royal Melbourne Institute of Technology (RMIT) have found that certain roads may cause a steady flow of vibrations at certain low frequencies which happens while driving on these surfaces. These low vibrations may lull the brain and body, relaxing you and making you sleepy.

> *"We believe that what's happening is that the sensory input that's coming from the vibrations is starting to synchronize the brain waves and put the brain into sleep," said Robinson, head of the psychology department at RMIT.*

The frequency of these car seat vibrations resembled those of theta waves, which are the brain waves connected with entering the sleep state. An electroencephalogram (EEG) is a test that detects electrical activity in your brain. As shown in EEG's, as subjects drift off to sleep, theta wave activity increases.

As mentioned in the commandments of roadtripping, if you doze off (EVEN ONCE!), pull over at a rest stop if nearby, or find a Walmart parking lot for your nap. Falling asleep at the wheel, even for a second, can disorient you and cause an accident that injures you, your passengers, and innocent people in other cars. Don't risk your life, it's not worth it.

INTERACTING WITH POLICE OFFICERS

These may seem like common sense for most, but the smallest things make all of the difference. I've been pulled over more times than I can even remember. I've had my car searched, etc., and have all kinds of stories...possibly because I've had a range of sketchy vehicles from the old Mercury Grand Marquis that resembled an old Crown Victoria police receptor, to an old BMW with 20-inch chrome rims. (Hey, I was young.) Maybe I looked suspicious, who knows— my point is that I've noticed patterns and can proudly say I received warnings at least 40% of the time. Now that I've got your attention...follow these tips:

1. Remember that police officers put their lives on the line for us every day. Even though you aren't happy about getting pulled over, they are just doing their job. Imagine if they didn't pull you over for speeding, if they did not enforce the law, driving anywhere would be risking your life. Without them, there would be so many reckless drivers flying by you going over 100 mph or more (we've all seen crazy drivers who put others at risk because of their immaturity or lack of responsibility.) With all of that being said, be grateful , own up to whatever you did or seek to find out what you did wrong with an open mind. Always be nice! I have found that by simply being nice, police officers may be more inclined to give you a warning because the majority of people can be so bitter after being pulled over. Now this shouldn't be fake, genuinely appreciate them doing their job, and you may

get a break. If you get a ticket, it shouldn't change your respectful behavior.

2. Always look out in the police officers best interest. What I mean by this is when you're getting pulled over, don't be selfish or clueless and just stop somewhere that slows traffic flow or puts them in danger when they try to approach your vehicle. When you see sirens, always use your turn signals and look for the safest place for both of you to pull over. If this means driving another quarter of a mile, as long as you have your turn signal on and are slowing down they will know your intentions and respect them. Try to pull off a main road, into a parking lot, or far enough into the grass off the interstate, slightly turned away from the road to provide more cover in a sense.

3. Be aware. Clearly if you are getting pulled over, the officer is going to ask for your license and registration, so get it ready before they approach the vehicle. Don't be scrambling to find your documents when they walk up (imagine how that would look to them). If you can't get them out in time, simply open your window and sit there with both hands on the wheel. Once the police officer greets you and requests the documents, you can tell them where the documents are and slowly reach for them. If you do this very quickly you could make them uncomfortable (think about how many people have reached for a gun and harmed a police officer while being pulled over in the past).

4. Simply put yourself in their shoes, treat them the way you would want to be treated and handle yourself accordingly. If you get a ticket, accept it , put it away and you can deal with it long after you return from your road trip! Don't let it affect anything! Be grateful nothing serious happened and you're still taking an epic road trip!

Chapter 12: The nitty gritty

"Life is either a daring adventure or nothing at all."

—*Helen Keller*

Chapter 13

A TASTE OF FREEDOM

Traveling as a teenager

My sweet, customized ride in Sarasota, Florida

As a young teen we all dreamed of freedom, anxiously awaiting the day that would take off in a car on our own for the first time. When that day came, it became a turning point in our lives as it allowed us **independence** and freedom to do whatever we wished.

I was a shy but adventurous 16-year-old and the whole drive-yourself-anywhere experience had just hit me—it was like an entire new world. Having a summer birthday in June, I ended up being one of the oldest in my class and one of the first to begin driving. I became the unofficial chauffeur as every other kid in my school would ask me for rides. I would zip around in my old Mercury Grand Marquis with 7-8 high school kids strategically squeezed and piled throughout the boat of a car, while the car sat low and the V8 kept us rumbling along from stop to stop. Sure, I was a free taxi for everyone, and I rarely got gas money, but I didn't care—I was driving my own car!

There came a point where my "big old car" was transformed into a vehicle with a completely different personality. One of my neighborhood friends had noticed that my car looked like an old-style police cruiser, so we decided to spray paint the entire car black and take advantage of this (in legal ways of course). We mounted an old CB radio on the dashboard and wired it to a loud speaker in the grill of the car. You can only imagine the things we would do, from messing with pedestrians through the loudspeaker, to pulling up to parties and watching kids scatter like ants in an anthill, and much more.

This vehicle was so much more than just a car; it was freedom, allowing me to discover not only what was around me, but what was within, as I had more and more experiences on my own.

Gradually, more and more of my friends got cars, also. We would still ride around together, just divided up into two or more cars. We even reached a low point where we began to play Demolition Derby with all of our old beat-up vehicles, using a parking lot as our course and slamming into each other. With each jolt, we sustained new dent after new dent.

One day, we were sitting outside looking at my ugly, spotty, beat-up car and my friend asked if he could carve his name into my car. With permission, he proceeded to walk over and begin to carve his name using a key, on the side of my Grand Marquis, into the spray paint. It wasn't long before this became a phenomenon. Soon, I would have at least a handful of people every day ask to sign my car! While many were kind enough to ask permission, oftentimes I would come out of the grocery store and find new "auto-graphs."

I was fortunate to have several friends who lived in the same neighborhood. To the left, down the street, was one crew, while there was another on the other far side. Ironically, I was isolated somewhere in the middle, and I always tended to be the loner. I'll refer to them as the east side and west side. I would often try to unite the east side and west side to play together, but they would typically stay on their own sides of the neighborhood and I would try to balance my time between both. On the west side, I had friends named Kyle and Jason. Jason was older and seemed to know everything about electronics, mechanics, and computers. One time he helped me with a custom installation of lights on my dashboard that I could turn on with a switch he installed. This set-up was all custom and very impressive; I couldn't believe that after only a few hours, I had different colored lights on my dash and floor to light up my car like teen night at a dance club. Can you imagine how much of a game changer this was for a 16-year-old? Of course I proudly displayed the light show during every date I went on.

My friend and I would drive to the beach and meet tourist girls, using our terribly original line, "Are you from around here?" It was great fun to show them around the city and get to show off my car and custom lights at the same time. We would usually end up back at a scenic area, showing off the beauty of our beloved city of Sarasota.

One evening my friend Mirza and I went on a double date with two girls on vacation and we ended up at a beautiful beach. Mirza and his date were sitting in his fancy white-on-white Toyota Celica with a body kit and rims, while I sat in my hoopty-hoop with the other young lady. Seeking to impress, I said , "Check this out." I proceeded to flip the switch and my car illuminated like Christmas lights. It was beautiful in its own misplaced way.

Just as I leaned a little closer to her, she said, "What's that smell?" I too smelled it, a slight smoky smell, but I ignored it at first.

"I don't know," I said, sounding as unconcerned as possible.

"It smells like smoke—look!" I turned my head to see smoke begin pouring out of my dashboard! I jumped out of the car and went to check under the hood. The entire light system was ablaze!

It was a tragedy. My car become ablaze, although we eventually put the fire out...but the dates had already come to an end.

About six months later, my friends Zach and Mirza and I decided to take our first mini road trip together to Miami. We took off for Miami Beach, a 3.5 hour expedition including a long stretch of the route literally named "Alligator Alley." We may not have calculated expenses accurately, and left Sarasota with about $120 between us. We hoped to find a cheap place to sleep or just crash on the bench seats of the car.

Right on schedule, we arrived in the vicinity of our paradise destination. I remember rolling down the window to ask a car next to us, "Where is South Beach?"

They shouted, "You're on it, dude!"

It was a different world. We walked around among Rolls Royces and Ferraris, beautiful people all around, and overheard more Spanish in an hour than I had heard in my entire life. As we moved our car from one side of South Beach to the other, we soon realized that gas was to eat up the majority of our funds. Hungry, we went to Subway and ordered a sub, asking for extra vegetables on the side to form a pathetic little salad. This was our dinner.

We continued exploring and met a group of girls from Ohio, there for vacation. Jackpot! We now had people to hang out with. They also were under 18 and couldn't get in the clubs, so we walked the key together. Eventually, they went back to their hotel and invited us to sleep in the lobby. Yes, you heard me, the lobby...where you are not supposed to sleep; the area where you transition to get to your rooms or vehicles.

Out of all the warm 80-90 degree days and nights that Miami is famous for, this was not one of them. It was freezing! We shivered in our seats without jackets or any blankets. We struggled to get a little sleep before we would have to head back. Soon enough it was 4am and we decided to get on the road. Little did we know the journey was far from over.

A car GPS did not exist at this time, so we had to rely on a MapQuest print-out. A little sheet of paper directed us turn by turn how to get to

Miami; for some reason, we failed to print one for the return trip and had sadly thrown away the original.

We drove through the streets of Miami, often turning the wrong way on one-way streets (as we learned the hard way) and eventually found our way to the interstate. I drove while they slept while I tried to follow signs. Four hours later, one of them woke up and said, "Aren't we there yet?"

I knew we were lost and almost out of gas. We turned to each other with looks of serious doubt. We did a U-turn and passed a sign, "Everglades City 21 miles." Looking at the fuel gauge clearly on the red, we prayed for our reserve to get us there. We drove down this two-lane road without ever seeing another car, vultures hovering above us and the Everglades all around us.

It really was that dramatic as we thought that at any moment the car would give its final engine turn, quit, and leave us stranded. Who wants to leave a car and walk through the Florida wilderness (where black bears, panthers, and countless alligators live)? Somehow we made it to a gas station in Everglades City and ultimately all the way home after getting good directions from a Haitian man with dreads.

Moral of the story: This trip was the first time I could truly test myself and be outside of my comfort zone, completely self-reliant, without anyone to turn to. This, my first roadtrip, expanded my small world through new experiences and challenges, leading to me gaining confidence as a 16-year-old with a story behind me.

How To Road Trip America

*Wild horses on the beach in Cumberland Island,
off the coast of South Georgia*

PART 3

> *"Living on Earth is expensive,
> but it does include a free trip
> around the sun every year."*
>
> *Unknown*

Chapter 14

ROUGHING IT!

This Chapter is for those who wish to be as resourceful as possible

Miss Bella debating getting back in her bed

This chapter is not for everyone; yet, many roadtrippers have big dreams but not big budgets. Only read this if you want to save as much money as possible and don't mind taking things to the extreme. There are three levels of roughing it. The 2nd and 3rd levels of roughing it are more extreme, and you must be careful and have common sense. I am simply teaching the best ways to do them, but do so at your own risk!

Roughing it is categorized in three parts. The first is a normal trip that involves hotels, and saves on expenses by bringing your own food. Level two is a little more involved. This consists of camping or couch surfing, rather than using hotels. Level three is your "roughest" scenario, although it doesn't ever have to have a negative connotation. It's simply the most adventurous and requires resourcefulness!

Level 1 Roughing It: #roughingitlevel1

This is the perfect scenario when you have some funds but are trying not to spend money on what you feel could be deemed "unnecessary." For many people, a bed in a room with A/C is necessary, so other ways to be frugal should be considered. If you won't sacrifice the comforts of a hotel, you can still find the cheapest lodging possible, and save money on food. I recommend bringing a big cooler so that you can pack and bring food for breakfast, lunch, and snacks.

Level 2 Roughing It: #roughingitlevel2

This is a little more advanced and requires a little more tolerance. This consists of the same cooler-packing plan, but adds in some new lodging strategies. Instead of cheap hotels, your target is campgrounds! You'll need a tent or camper, unless you decide to forgo the camping and choose to couch surf (staying free at residences—more details to follow).

Level 3 Roughing It: #roughingitlevel3

This is the ultimate economy plan and requires the greatest amount of strategy. Though you can still try to couch surf, I would plan on relying entirely on yourself. If you happen to secure a couch for the evening, that's simply a bonus! For Level 3 Roughing It, this is the worst case

Chapter 14: Roughing it!

scenario: homeless on the open road. However, it's not as hard as it may seem and can actually be an adventure in itself!

All you need for this one is your vehicle, a cooler, pillow, and blankets. At Level 3, you obviously sleep in your car and your safest spot (other than a campground) which will be a Walmart parking lot, preferably a 24-hour Walmart. You'll find other fellow parking lot campers and see a small number of people coming in and out of the store throughout the night. The parking lot is under surveillance and that will help give you peace of mind, but of course you must keep your windows rolled mostly all the way up and your doors locked. You can also access the restrooms any time of the night which will give you comfort. I would recommend parking more towards a front corner where you're in front enough for safety yet far enough away where there's not constant traffic around your vehicle.

Your next best friend will be Starbucks, which are typically very strategically placed as you don't find them in higher crime areas but usually generally safer areas of the city. If you have trouble sleeping or don't feel comfortable in the Walmart parking lot, head to Starbucks. As soon as the clock hits 5am, 6am or 6:30am (depending on location), the coffee shop will open. Also, throughout the day when you just want to relax indoors, you can always go take it easy at a Starbucks and plan your next stop.

Roughing it does not have to always feel rough, by the way. Again, having a successful strategy is all about being resourceful. For example, a 24/7 gym is another great asset for roughing it. Chain gyms such as LA Fitness can be found in most major cities across America, so if you're the type that will be roughing it often, I'd recommend getting a membership prior to your trip. Another option is to get a membership at your local YMCA. Over 2,600 Y locations around the country participate in honoring your local membership as a "national" membership and you can use their facilities.

Here's a good strategy: Research locations for both Walmart and your gym in the area you plan to sleep. This way you can sleep in the Walmart parking lot, using the store's restroom the night before for brushing your teeth. In the morning, you can either use the Walmart restroom again or head over to the gym. (You get bonus points if you work out before you shower!) You don't need to buy breakfast since you'll have what you need in your cooler.

Keep in mind that you can go to the gym any time they are open (and most open early and close late). So a gym membership can be your home-away-from-home for a hot shower when you are living out of your car. If you don't have a membership or can't find your gym where you are, but you are in desperate need of a shower, most offer a one-day pass for $5-$20, depending on the establishment.

If you are organized enough, you can maintain this cycle more easily than you may imagine. Walmart to sleep, Starbucks for a safe haven during the day or evening, and a gym for your shower needs. You can also purchase things to make life easier, such as a door netting to keep bugs out. It goes over the windows to allow you to crack the windows just enough for some air but still closed enough for safety reasons. You can also get a fan, and anything else that makes you more comfortable because your car will be off the entire night. Do not try to leave the car running— it's a long time to idle and you wouldn't want to risk carbon monoxide poisoning if you're in an enclosed area or your exhaust pipe is blocked, so just turn the car off.

If you are doing this because of lack of funding, know this—money comes and goes, and it will never define you. You may be in a time of transition. Many times taking a roadtrip is the perfect way to clear your mind, get re-energized, and become inspired to begin a new chapter in your life. It can help you gain self-confidence, too, and discover just how resourceful you really are.

Roadtrip Cost-Cutters

Packing your food

Your cooler has now become one of your most prized possessions. In fact, think about bringing an extra-large cooler. (If you don't have one, it can be an easy item to borrow from someone who won't need it while you are away.) You can pack the majority of your food and cut expenses drastically! If you pack milk and cereal for breakfast, bowls and silverware can be rinsed out immediately after. (Tip: almond milk keeps fresh considerably longer than regular milk) While on the road, you can replenish something you need by making a quick stop at a grocery store, avoiding the expense of restaurants as much as possible—only when it's in your budget and is likely to be an experience that's worth it.

Drafting

Have you ever watched professional racing? These drivers know all about drafting. You can reduce fuel consumption by following a truck, the bigger the better. This reduces the effect of drag and greatly increases your fuel economy. The closer you get, the better your miles-per-gallon increase. Keep in mind that nobody likes to be tailgated! You must always keep a **safe distance** and simply enjoy a slightly slower pace behind a semi-truck in the slow lane. If they change lanes, don't follow them as you want it to be natural and considerate above all else. Remain at your proper slow-lane speed and soon enough you will end up behind another truck to draft behind. Drive safely and responsibly, this is just meant to make you aware that if you drive in the slow lane you can benefit with increased mileage because you'll probably end up behind trucks the entire way.

You Mean I Can Sleep on Your Couch?

You actually can! It's called *couch surfing* and there is an official website called www.couchsurfing.org. This site allows you to create a profile and travel America (and in other countries) and stay on people's couches or in a spare bedroom. The website does a background check on each member (who must pay a verification fee) and provides a safe environment to connect potential hosts with travelers.

The network allows travelers to meet locals and learn about their way of life and city, while locals get to provide hospitality and meet (adventurous!) people from different areas and backgrounds. The range of these services depends on what both host and traveler want. Communicate clearly! Many hosts want to spend some time with you and hear your story, while others are just willing to give you a place to crash and help them build their profile with a good recommendation.

I have some friends now in other parts of the world because I hosted couch surfers when I was living in Miami. My roommate and I hosted many men and women since it was a popular tourist destination. It was a positive, rewarding experience and we learned so much about different cultures. We made many international friends whom I keep in touch with even today.

Nothing is 100% risk-free, but there are several safety elements built in to the website. They do a professional background check prior to approving hosts so you can be sure you are not staying with someone with a criminal background. You can also do research on the person that will potentially host you. Their profile gives you an overall idea of who they are. You can read reviews from previous guests on their profile and even reach out to previous guests to see what their experience was like. Lastly, after your stay, you both get to write a review about the person. Neither one wants a bad review, which increases the likelihood that both the host and traveler are nice and that the stay is a positive experience.

Couch surfing is an amazing resource and I think everyone should take advantage. However, I highly recommend doing so with a friend and not alone. Once in a while, a female couch surfer we hosted would tell us of her prior experiences where a male host made them feel a little uncomfortable, or maybe even being somewhat suggestive. You have the option to request that you only stay with members of the same sex, or couples. In my own experience as a surfing traveler, it was sometimes challenging to find a host because women were not open to hosting one male traveler, while some men were only open to hosting female travelers. This is just generally speaking, and I did have many couples willing to host me. The website is a great thing as long as you follow these steps:

1. Create a profile.

2. Try to attend *couchsurfing* events prior to traveling. They have meet-and-greets, etc.

3. If you can, offer to host a traveler or two and build up those references if you hope to find a host in the near future. A couple of good reviews go a long way to having a trustworthy profile.

Chapter 14: Roughing it!

Put yourself in a host's shoes, then look at *what does my profile convey?*

4. Reach out to different hosts in advance and see which ones follow up. Many simply don't get to their messages right away, and so reaching out in advance makes a big difference.

5. Communicate clear dates and expectations. Think this through. Are you deathly allergic to long-haired cats? Better check out everything you need to check on ahead of time.

6. Do your research. For more peace of mind, reach out to former travelers they hosted. If you hear a bad reference, simply tell the host you changed your mind or found someone else. Be careful who you stay with. Stick with members of the same sex or older couples. Use common sense.

7. Always travel with a friend or two.

8. During your stay, be mindful and courteous so you will definitely get a good review from your host. It is not uncommon to leave them a small gift, nothing major, just a thank-you.

Take a chance, try it out, and you will have a memorable and, most likely, a very good experience. As I mentioned, the couch surfing network is an amazing resource as it connects travelers with those who want to share a small slice of life. It allows you to make friends and feel at home while away from home. Not to mention, hosts in this network must agree that your stay will always be free!

In conclusion, your trip is what you make of it and there are many ways to cut costs to have an amazing trip with memorable experiences.

Chapter 15

THE ART OF CONVERSATION

Going Deeper

Making new friends at the La Jolla cove in San Diego, California

When you are traveling with a friend, partner or others, you will find that sharing the journey for long stretches of time provides phenomenal opportunities for connection. Understand and appreciate that people have different ways of communicating, different comfort levels of intimacy, and different needs for engaging with others.

Introverts and extroverts have different conversational needs; however, it can be easy for everyone to enjoy conversation through simply being self-aware and appreciating those around you. After all, you all chose to take a trip together! Here are a few communication rules to help you know how to make this comfortable for all personality types:

1. Ironically, I will start with this: Silence is golden. Don't feel the need to always fill the silence or feel obligated to entertain anyone. It is normal for there to be stretches of silence during a roadtrip to relax, enjoy the views or simply reflect.

2. Be a good listener! This stuff may seem like common sense to some; however, many are not as aware. Listening is an incredibly powerful way to connect with another person while also asking deep questions. Even if you like to talk, make sure you give other people a chance to share what is on their mind, and do not interrupt them. Take turns talking and listening to each other's stories using active listening. Respond appropriately and at the right time. There's nothing more frustrating than trying to talk to someone who tries to dominate every conversation, asking a question only to quickly interrupt your answer and then turn the conversation back on them.

   If you are extroverted or "a talker," don't take advantage of having a captive audience to go on and on and on and on rambling. It may look like they are listening, but it's always better to take turns speaking and listening. Finish your story and points and give others a chance to talk.

   After someone tells a personal story, be genuinely interested and ask follow-up questions to learn more. Then you can take turns if you have something to add or share. Instantly, you will be perceived as a better listener and conversationalist. Don't just talk about yourself the entire time; ask the people you're with questions equally or more than you answer them.

3. When you need a break, speak up! It can be tiring if there's one person who doesn't realize everyone is zoned out. They miss the signals that others are zoning out and that they seem to want some quiet time. There's a time and a place for everything, and sometimes the other passengers need a break from questions

Chapter 15: The art of conversation

and storytelling. Simply be aware and let things be organic. One person's sense of balance between conversation and quiet time is usually different from the next person's, so it is okay to let someone know what you need. Saying something like, "I'm just going to rest for a while," or " I'm just going to zone out and enjoy this view," will give you space. Simply communicate, explain what you need.

4. Communicate openly. Be straightforward and communicate. It's only uncomfortable when you're focused on someone else and have a need for validation. Just be yourself, be aware, let things be organic and enjoy the trip. As the driver, you can occasionally ask if anyone needs to stop for a break, even it is has not yet been the full two hours, If you are a passenger, don't stress yourself out waiting for the driver to pull over for a break. Communicate that you need a break, whatever your reason.

During the ride, be responsible for being comfortable, whether it is requesting that someone roll up their window or that you stop so you can get a blanket out of the trunk. I'm sure you'll be comfortable enough with everyone if you're taking a roadtrip together; however, if you're not as familiar with each other you should still just be yourself.

You can drive anywhere with anyone as long as you follow the guidelines and roadtrip commandments. The only time people will get frustrated with one another and have a bad roadtrip experience is if they are not following the guidelines and roadtrip commandments. For example: If you don't follow the roadtrip commandments and you choose to drive 12 hours in a day, and don't arrive at your first destination until 2am, and then repeat it the next day, do you think you will actually be able to enjoy the journey, let alone even stand the people next to you?

There's no way! You will rob each other of the ability to strengthen relationships as you will all be angry and bitter, trying to stay awake on the road and anxious to get to your destination because the journey will be painful! Why will it be painful? Because you made it that way! You put yourself in a tiny vehicle with three other people and made it feel like a prison on wheels for 12 hours. It's what you make of it, just like anything in life and that is the exact purpose of this book! There's a right and a wrong way to roadtrip and this book will show you how to do it right.

Just be willing to follow the guidelines and commandments and then everyone can remain rested, relaxed, and in the right frame of mind to enjoy the journey and bonding interactions which will allow for strengthening relationships and once-in-a-lifetime experiences.

Chapter 15: The art of conversation

"Travel far enough, you meet yourself"

—*David Mitchell*

Chapter 16

THE ART OF BEING

*Roadtrips are Catalysts for Personal Growth
Through Mindfulness, Uninterrupted Thinking, and Self-Reflection*

Del Mar Beach, California

As mentioned previously, roadtrips offer an array of psychological benefits and are huge catalysts for personal growth. This time with yourself in new environments is crucial as it encourages self-discovery on a fundamental level, while providing perspective within different experiences. Throughout the trip you will be forced to live in the present and come across many lessons that will allow growth. Being free from any stress or obligation on the open road allows you to think freely and deeply, a therapeutic benefit that promotes healing from any past trauma.

> *"The secret of health for both mind and body is not to mourn for the past, worry about the future, or anticipate troubles, but to live in the present moment wisely and earnestly."*
> —Buddha

MINDFULNESS

According to the formal definition, mindfulness is a state of mind achieved by focusing one's attention on the present moment. Rather than dwelling on the past or living in the future, it is focused on the now. Many of us tend to live in the future in anticipation of when we "get there." "I'll relax and spend more time with family once I get that raise," or "I'll take that trip to visit my mother once my house is completed." We must always remember that we are not promised tomorrow and that all we really have is the present moment. We are truly the only animal that is capable of living in the past or future, any other living creature lives in the present moment, experiencing and letting it flow. Of course, this awareness and intelligence is one of the many characteristics that set us apart from animals. There is a time and a place to reminisce on the past for different reasons or think of the future for planning purposes; however; the majority of your time should be in the present.

When one is always forward thinking, they cannot truly be happy and time will fly by as they focus on a point in the future that they never reach. Living in the future causes anxiety and robs you of the present while living in the past will often lead to feelings of depression because it seems better than the present.

"Some people die at 25 and aren't buried until 75."
-Benjamin Franklin

Studies show that by simply focusing one's attention on the present, there are numerous health benefits such as: improved well-being, improved mood, less perceived stress, less anxiety and depression. A study found that people on average spend nearly half their time (46.7%) thinking about something other than what they are doing.

Simply focus on directing your attention on the now; don't let this moment slip away as you will truly never have it again. Here are some exercises to help you focus on the present and being mindful:

1. Let go of judgments about yourself or others and focus on what is going on around you.

2. Savor the moment, the precious little things from seeing your child's smile in the backseat to a butterfly flying by or simply a nice cool breeze. This world is a magnificent one and can impress you every day by simply walking outside, opening up your eyes or simply feeling and listening to what is going on around you.

3. Breathe deeply and slowly. Your breathing directly affects your nervous system and has the ability to both relax your body and mind to be more fully receptive.

4. Words are powerful because they are able to reach us on a subconscious level. Try an affirmation such as: "I am present and fully aware of this moment in all of its greatness and beauty."

5. Take a walk in nature and listen to the sounds around you, the smells, the sun glistening through the branches and every little thing going on around you.

Mindfulness is simply self-regulation of attention, with openness and acceptance.

BE GRATEFUL

Before I get to the power of gratefulness I want to put things in perspective. Let's first acknowledge how stress directly affects the body in drastic ways. We all know this and it cannot be denied as science has proven it to be true. Now, with that being said, we know that stress is all perception that comes from our own minds. Your mind is immensely powerful, beyond what you have ever imagined.

Now after acknowledging how powerful one simple feeling can be and how it can affect the mind and body, we must also recognize that there are others that have just as much impact, though in positive ways.

One feeling that has the power to drastically change our lives to the same degree, if not more, is that of being grateful. As you have recognized the negative, mental effects of stress, you now must appreciate that the mindset of being grateful can have just as much influence on your mind and body in positive, amazing ways.

My point is, by simply shifting your mentality to one of gratefulness, you will transform your entire life as your brain changes, your attitude shifts and you grow.

Let's face it, most of us reading this book live in America or are blessed with the resources to have an interest in taking American roadtrips. That alone means you most likely don't have to worry about finding your next meal, or having a roof over your head when you return from your trip. If you're in the lowest 5% standard of living economically in America, that has been shown to be the equivalent of the top 5% in countries such as India. Chances are you have a job that provides enough income, you have countless opportunities ahead, and you have your health, along with family and friends who love you.

On a side note, keep in mind that it actually doesn't even have anything to do with money as some of the poorest societies in the world have the happiest people. Happiness and fulfillment typically comes down to the same four components across the board:

Chapter 16: The art of being

1. **Self-improvement-** Discovering yourself on a fundamental level, loving yourself and finding a sense of purpose; striving to pursue your path and dreams.

2. **Relationships-** Valuing your friends and loved ones while genuinely appreciating daily interactions with others throughout each day.

3. **Giving back-** There are many ways to give back: donating time, money or goods, helping others, simply striving to better serve without expectations of anything in return.

4. **New experiences-** Living in the moment and enjoying the small things, butterflies flying by, trying new foods, traveling, driving home a new way, trying a new activity. This simply encompasses mindfulness, growth and variety.

Your happiness and fulfillment is generally created in taking those four parts within the right balance—in creating whatever lifestyle you choose.

We all have endless things to be grateful for; however, we often tend to focus on the lack of what we still want rather than what we already have. Focusing on the lack is what causes your perceived level of stress, which is completely unnecessary. You can now begin to see that with a simple shift in thought, living in the present and reflecting occasionally on all of your blessings, how much happiness and joy this can bring you.

Gratefulness Changes Your Brain

In a study, a research team from the University of Indiana led by Prathik Kini worked with 43 subjects that suffered from depression and anxiety. Over the course of three months, half the group was required to write letters of thanks to those in their lives and brain scans were taken. After the study, the brain scans showed that there were profound and long lasting neural changes that occurred and the associated participants felt many more feelings associated with being grateful. Overall, being grateful caused lasting effects on the brain as it synchronized activation in various brain regions and showed stimulation of the brain's reward pathways and hypothalamus. Comparable to antidepressant drugs, gratitude boosts levels of the neurotransmitter serotonin and activates the brainstem to produce dopamine—both of which are considered your brain's "happy" chemicals.

- Gratitude can free you from toxic emotions

- Being grateful will allow love to begin to flow more freely

- Gratefulness will change your mindset and change your brain over time

**Trying to think of things you are grateful for forces you to focus on the positive aspects of your life.
This simple act increases serotonin production
in the anterior cingulate cortex of the brain.**

REMINISCING

Nostalgia is typically related to regret or depression, though neuroscience has proven it to be a mood enhancer. As long as you're not living in the past as I mentioned previously, there is nothing wrong with remembering all the amazing memories you have created. Though you may miss these past events, thinking about them causes your hippocampus to reward you and actually enhances your mood. After all, you are creating these memories to not only be experienced in the moment but also remembered! The only downside of reminiscing is if it comes at the cost of living in the present and missing what is going on around you, or if you're spending the majority of your time in the past.

As long as you are mindful and live in the present, there is nothing wrong with reflecting back on memories over the years and having conversations with friends or family members about them. Remember, think back and relive but don't do so at the expense of new amazing moments.

REFLECTING

Reflecting and reminiscing are similar in that they both involve looking back on past experiences or events; however, rather than simply enjoying the memories, reflecting is about finding the significance and the associated impact in these events on your life. It's important to address any negative events or behaviors in the past to break them down, rather than sweep them under the carpet. Though this can be uncomfortable the deeper you dig, it will get easier and eventually you'll feel a weight lifted once you break through the wall.

1. Be honest with yourself
2. Think about your values and principles
3. Notice behavioral patterns
4. Think about your own behavior in different situations and beliefs

Why did you act that way?

How did you feel?

Where did those feelings stem from?

Understanding yourself on a fundamental level will directly increase your self-awareness, which will improve your understanding of others and, therefore, make you more patient and accepting, while directly changing your brain for the better.

> *"The Essence of knowledge is self-knowledge."*
> —*Pluto*

SELF DISCOVERY

I know this chapter is deep, but it's necessary and this section will bring it all together. Self-discovery is crucial for a happy and fulfilled life and there truly isn't any way around it. Life is truly a journey and roadtrips are symbolic of this, allowing you the time outside of your daily distractions to really face yourself and begin, or continue learning, to love yourself.

Every single one of us has unique gifts and a purpose, and it's up to us to begin our journey of self-discovery, learning the qualities that we inherently have within us. The more you dig, the more you understand yourself which provides direct clarity in your life. If you don't know who you are, how can you recognize a good partner when one comes along? If you don't know yourself, how can you know what career is the best fit for you?

This unfortunately isn't taught in school, though it is the highest form of knowledge. Many of us go through life never diving below the surface for an array of reasons and then never truly know what we want out of life or find that sense of purpose. It's never too late, begin your journey and dig deep.

Questions for Self-Discovery

1. What matters most to me?

2. What are my personal gifts, natural talents?

3. What are the operating principles in my life?

4. What qualities do I see myself having?

5. How do I think others see me?

6. What three words describe me best?

7. Am I more introverted or extroverted, what is my personality like?

8. What am I passionate about?

9. When I'm in emotional or physical pain, how do I deal with this?

10. What are my values?

11. What do I love to do and want to do more of?

12. What do I want to do less of?

13. What would a perfect day in my life look like?

14. How do I feel about my last mistake and what did I learn from it?

15. Do I acknowledge when I make mistakes?

16. Do I often make excuses and why?

17. What motivates and inspires me?

18. Am I holding onto something that I can let go?

19. How am I censoring what I think or feel?

20. What limiting beliefs are impacting my life?

21. How do I sabotage my life?

22. What would I attempt if I knew I could do anything?

"Once a year, go someplace you've never been before."

—Dalai Lama

Chapter 17

ON THE TRIP HOME

Reflecting on your journey and cherishing your memories

*Bella enjoying the view and reflecting on her life,
somewhere in southern Colorado*

The trip home is simply the second half of your trip—with a little planning, it should be just as interactive and exciting as the first half. As previously mentioned, try to take a different route, depending on the trip type, or at least make different stops on this leg of your trip.

Ways to change up the return trip include: driving on different roads, stopping at different attractions, trying other restaurants, visiting different attractions or using different kinds of lodging. For example, if you stayed on someone's couch in Panama City, Florida, as your second day's stop, you could look around the area and find a reasonable hotel room on the beach to stay at on your return trip, giving you that to look forward to during the rest of your journey, or even stay in a different city in the same general area.

Aside from the experiences you'll have on the way back, as you get closer to home, it's a great time to review all the highlights of your trip—the good, interesting, and the hilarious. Remember and discuss with your trip mates the parts you each enjoyed the most and you can even put together an online album to document your epic trip on Facebook. I recommend creating a Facebook album and naming it whichever theme you chose to brand the trip. You can post the pictures in a timeline sequence form the time you left until you return so the album tells a story. You can choose to set the album as private and simply allow it to be a reference for personal memories or insight for future trips, or you can make it public so your families and friends can see the highlights of your adventure! There is much value in creating these albums. It not only gives you a beautiful virtual photo album of your amazing trip, but it also gives you a way to quickly reminisce when you need a little boost or want to reflect on those times. The photos can also serve as documentation of your favorite spots. You can use them as a reference when you want to go back, or when you want to give someone some good ideas as they plan to go somewhere that you have already experienced.

You can use Yelp to record your favorite experiences, through posting a review for whichever park or restaurant you really enjoyed. If you are ever in that area again, your Yelp reviews will serve as a reference that you can refer back to. Trust me, if you don't do this, you'll regret it later when you find yourself asking, *What was the name of that amazing restaurant?* or, *What was that one park hidden away in the mountains?* Build your list across the nation and you'll be able to have these similar experiences again or share them with loved ones!

Chapter 17: On the trip home

HASHTAGS FOR SHARING

Let's build our roadtrip community through sharing discoveries and places for key experiences together! Use #hashtags on Instagram! Feel free to hashtag throughout your epic adventure as you post on social media at the end of your trip! Here are recommendations to build a like-minded community and share experiences:

#Howtoroadtrip #Roadtripping #Chooseyourdreamadventure #modernroadtrip #epicroadtrip #goingsomewhere #itsaboutthejourney #8steps #Usingthemaps #commandmentsofroadtripping #plannedtrip #unplannedtrip #roadtripcommandments #HowToRoadTripAmerica #Cruisinsolo #cruisinwithBae #crewcruisin #cruisinwiththefam #planningmyepicroadtrip #BreakRitual #Roughingitlevel1 #Roughingitlevel2 #Roughingitlevel3

How To Road Trip America

Chapter 18

FOLLOW YOUR HEART

My first Cross Country Roadtrip as an Adult

Sunset Cliffs, San Diego, California

We all must learn how to follow our hearts in creating our happiness and fulfillment within the lives we want. Years ago, I personally chose to give up stability for love and adventure and I'm glad that I made the choice that I did.

I was in my mid-to-late twenties and working at a restaurant located in a local high-end hotel and resort, and I was just beginning to figure out my entrepreneurial path. Despite having a great restaurant resume, I stepped back from serving to take a barback position. My hope was that I would learn bartending and eventually take a bartending position at this high-end establishment, while getting started as a personal trainer in the mornings. I stepped away from more money as a server to learn this new skill and embrace this new potential opportunity as a barback. It was hard work! I had forgotten the true work required of these positions in the hospitality industry and would often need to get hyped up on caffeine in order to manage my workload in such a busy environment.

There was a beautiful girl that would come in with her family and they would often sit at the bar and have dinner. I always had an eye on her, even though I knew I couldn't approach her in a romantic manner. It was against company policy, so I had to sit back and settle for occasional small talk. She had a nice family and was very intelligent in our brief conversations. I couldn't help but hope for an opportunity to talk to her a little more and possibly invite her out.

One night, I got cut early and finished everything. Normally I would be scrambling to get through the exit the second I was done, but not on this particular night. The Beautiful Girl was there with her family and I was almost disappointed that I was cut early. I went back in the kitchen for a few minutes and then took a deep breath and decided to go back out behind the bar one last time. I stepped out and acted busy for a moment before giving a final glance her direction. It was then she made eye contact and motioned me to come to her. I tried to play it cool as I slowly walked over and struck up a conversation. She told me she was new to Sarasota, and I offered to show her around sometime. It was a very brief encounter, but I did manage to get her number.

We began to hang out and it seemed perfect. We had a lot of fun together and I soon began to learn more about her career and how she was only in Sarasota for a limited amount of time. As time went on, she extended her time in the area and we moved in together.

Time went by and everything was great between us. We explored Sarasota and the west coast of Florida as I showed her key spots that I knew about from growing up in the area. Over the course of a few months, she began to mention how she couldn't wait to travel again. I also shared my dreams of being mobile and my plan on getting there. I told her I would gladly leave to go with her and would work to get myself in a position to do so—I began to make big moves in that direction.

Income was a stumbling block because I had been sacrificing income in order to have more creative time to figure out my entrepreneurial path, and also so that I could eventually take a bartending position and finally get my certification as a personal trainer as well. It was a period of much transition but I knew that it would be worth the sacrifice and hard work. The step back in order to take two forward left me in a financial position where I didn't have any money saved.

Two of the bartenders at work had left and the company had begun training me to finally take one of these bartending positions.

It wasn't long before I came to a fork in the road. I knew that my girlfriend wanted to continue with traveling. I also wanted to move, as well. It soon came down to either staying and starting to make more income as a bartender in the evenings and personal trainer in the mornings, or scraping up any money that I could and taking a chance, leaving with my girlfriend into the unknown, to go on an adventure.

I didn't think about it for long at all. It only took a moment to know where my heart was. If I chose to let her leave without me, I would always wonder "what if?" as long distance relationships typically don't do as well. And, like her, my wanderlust was growing stronger by the day, and my plan had been to do the same on my own within a couple of years after I had built more financial stability. I made my choice to go with her and my intention was set, so now it was just a matter of getting things in order to leave within a few weeks.

Once you are living out your intention to make a certain plan happen, you start to see creative ways to ensure that plan comes to fruition. I had to figure things out fast and decided to sell my beloved old 2003 Infiniti M45. Though this car was beginning to fall apart from all the miles of heavy driving it took, I had grown very fond of it. It was hard to part with as I had so many crazy memories from my college years, living in Miami and racing my roommate back from South Beach to Fort Lauderdale on weeknights at unmentionable speeds. And so many other memories. But, I knew it was time to let it go and move on to my next chapter. I decided to sell the car and purchase a bike from Walmart for less than $100. What a deal!

I rode this bicycle to work for a little while until it literally fell apart, after which point I purchased an old Cadillac from a family friend. I then used the car as collateral to get a loan, giving me some cash before we would take off.

Final adjustments were made as we packed up her car, "Lucy," the silver Nissan Sentra that was already missing a side view mirror, we took a chance and left on our first roadtrip across the country to live with each other in Los Angeles.

This first epic roadtrip showed us how well we worked together, while drastically changing our relationship for the better. We experienced life-changing moments together and had countless hours devoted to deep conversation.

I think the biggest factor that led to such a successful trip was the fact that we took our time and just enjoyed every step along the way. Nothing was forced. We were able to be ourselves and enjoy each moment together, while also dealing with any obstacles, one at a time. Overall, I am grateful for every special moment we shared together and all of the life changing experiences we had together.

The point of this story is to take chances, follow your heart and be intentional; truly live in the moment. This gives you the opportunity to enjoy all the gifts within the present. Each and every experience gives you an opportunity to grow. If you don't take chances, you'll always wonder, "What if?" After all, it's not the things we did but, rather, the things we didn't do that we regret the most.

Chapter 18: Follow your heart

"Wherever you go, go with all your heart."

—Confucius

Chapter 19

FUN FACTS

30 Fun Facts about Roadtrip-related Subjects

Somewhere in Death Valley, California

Fun Facts to Get You in the Mood, or to Share with your Travel Mates

1. US Route 20 is the longest road in the country. It runs through 12 states, from Oregon to Boston. Even though it is interrupted by Yellowstone National Park, it is 3,365 miles long!

2. The longest continual road is Route 6, running parallel to Route 20. It is 3,305 miles long and it takes you through 14 different states from California to Massachusetts.

3. The 33rd United States President, Harry Truman, and his wife Bess, took a 3-week roadtrip from Independence, Missouri, to New York without any secret service staff because they wanted to be "plain, private, citizens." They pumped their own gas and stopped at various diners and even got pulled over by a state trooper in Pennsylvania for driving too slow.

4. In 1960, the Pulitzer-Prize-winning author, John Steinbeck, took a cross country trek. After being diagnosed with a serious heart condition, he wanted to see the country one last time. Along with his 10-year-old poodle named Charlie, he drove in a GMC pickup with a camper mounted on the back that he named after Don Quixote's horse, "Rocinante." Upon his return, he wrote a book called, *Travels with Charlie* which became a New York Times Best Seller.

5. The two most popular roadtrip destinations in the nation are Yellowstone National Park (which is shared by Wyoming, Montana, and Idaho) and Walt Disney World in Florida.

6. Avoiding aggressive driving can increase your fuel economy by up to 33% on average.

7. According to a poll taken by roadtrip enthusiasts, *who* you go with is more important than *where* you go on a roadtrip.

Chapter 19: Fun facts

8. It would take 150 years to drive a car to the sun at normal highway speeds.

9. There are 182 places in the United States that have the word *Christmas* in their names.

10. San Francisco only has three cemeteries because, in 1937, residents passed a law saying that land was too valuable, so whole graveyards were actually dug up and moved outside the city limits. Many were relocated to the nearby town of Colma, which has more dead than living. This led to their city motto: "It's good to be alive in Colma."

11. Alaska has a longer coastline than all other 49 states put together, although it is the least populous state.

12. Georgia is the birthplace of miniature golf.

13. Canton Avenue, in Pittsburgh, Pennsylvania's Beechview neighborhood, is the steepest officially-recorded public street in the U.S. and, according to some sources, the world.

14. 28% of all the land in the United States is owned by the federal government. This translates to about 640 million acres. The western states have a much higher percentage of federally-owned land than other states do.

15. Harvard (Cambridge, Massachusetts) was the first university in the United States. It was founded in 1636 and is considered to be the second best university in the world. Eight American Presidents are alumni.

16. Manhattan's Chinatown has more Chinese residents than anywhere else in the Western hemisphere.

17. There are many fantastic beaches you can drive on in America, including the Outer Banks in North Carolina, Daytona Beach in Florida, Malaquite Beach in Texas, Silver Lake in Michigan, and Tierra del Mar in Oregon.

18. St. Augustine, Florida, established by Spanish explorer Don Pedro Menendez de Aviles in 1565, is the nation's oldest continuously occupied city, named after the patron saint of brewers.

19. Pensacola, Florida, was the first European-established colony in North America. It was settled in 1559 by Don Tristan De Luna.

20. There is enough water in Lake Superior to cover the entire landmass of North and South America in one foot of water.

21. Alabama is the only state whose official drink is an alcoholic beverage. Whiskey is their beverage of choice.

22. Arizona produces enough cotton each year to make two t-shirts for every American (599 million shirts).

23. If California were a country, it would have the 8th largest economy in the world, beating out Italy, Russia and India.

24. Although Colorado was meant to be a perfect rectangle, its purveyors wandered a little off course. There is a tiny kink in the western border that disqualifies it from being a pure rectangle.

25. In Alabama, it's illegal to walk around with an ice cream cone in your back pocket. This law was created when horse thieves wanted to steal horses without getting charged, since they only tempted the horse to follow them.

26. The marker at the summit of Lookout Mountain in Georgia claims you can, from there, view seven states: Tennessee, Kentucky, Virginia, South Carolina, North Carolina, Georgia and Alabama.

27. In Alaska, it's illegal to give alcohol to a moose. This law was created after a moose dipped into a local brewery's supply and gave quite a laugh to local residents.

28. Be wary when driving in Pennsylvania or West Virginia, especially, as that is where there is the highest risk of a car colliding with a deer.

29. Roadtrippers find the most unusual landmarks, for sure. Check out the World's Largest Thermometer, for example, in Baker, California. It keeps temperature, and is 134 ft. tall.

30. Driving literally across America is an impressive roadtrip goal. The northern-most route is the longest since you have to drive around the Great Lakes and the nation is wider at its top. A middle-America journey takes a little less time and decreases the risk of terrible weather. For a classic roadtrip across the country, try starting along the Atlantic coast in Charleston, South Carolina, and getting on Interstate 40 toward Los Angeles. At just under 2,500 miles, the trip clocks in at 36 hours driving time.

"May your adventures bring you closer together, even as they take you far away from home."

—*Trenton Lee Stewart*

Chapter 20

YOUR UPCOMING ADVENTURES

A final farewell and wishing you the best on your adventures/ final acknowledgments

Somewhere across the rolling plains of Georgia

I hope you have enjoyed this modern guide for the classic American roadtrip. It is meant to inspire you to learn all about these life-changing adventures and empower you to plan, take your own roadtrips, and create memories of a lifetime.

This book sets the stage by breaking down misconceptions and helping you recognize the vast benefits that roadtrips provide. To make the process as easy as possible, you now have all the tips you need to simplify the planning and packing processes. By following the guidelines, you can create quick seamless trips, from weekend getaways to longer cross-country adventures. *How to Roadtrip America* is also meant to be used during your roadtrips. It can serve as a guide and reference book to take with you on adventures—you can refer back to the commandments and access the resources listed.

A Journal, a Book, and More Resources Just for You!

There is a companion journal to follow the launching of this book, that is filled with inspirational quotes and room to write about your own adventures. You can use it to take notes of experiences, key places, restaurants, or anything else you want to remember along your trip. This can serve as another way to capture memories and important information as you travel. Check out the website for updates on when this will be available: howtoroadtripamerica.com

Subscribe to stay updated on each book in this series. One of the upcoming books will provide pre-planned, themed routes that will allow you to enjoy various experiences without having to do any planning yourself. Begin to apply the principles in this book in order to take roadtrips the right way and then you can use the upcoming book to choose and follow exact routes across the country and for additional insight.

I truly wish you all the best! Subscribe to the social media @howtoroadtripamerica as well as the blog at howtoroadtripamerica.com for updates and resources. Interact and share your thoughts and experiences! I want to hear about your epic adventures, especially your first trip!

Feel free to connect with me personally on social media:
Instagram: @jonsimos / Facebook: @jwsimos

Chapter 20: Your upcoming adventures

TAKE THESE 3 EASY STEPS:

1. Take one minute (literally) and follow the social media links and subscribe to the blog to stay connected.

2. Take this book and plan your first trip. Start small. Plan a 1-3 day trip in your surrounding area by following the base questions, packing lists, and commandments. Then you can try longer trips little by little.

3. Take your first trip and then come celebrate with us and share your experiences and help us build the road trip community.

You've got everything you need for a well-planned and memorable trip. I'm looking forward to hearing about all of your adventures and seeing you on the road!

Acknowledgments

A special thank you to my older Brother, Paul Simos, for believing in this project and funding the costs in the beginning to allow me to get going, without even a second thought. Also thank you to everyone in my family, for initially getting me started on these crazy trips at a young age while also always being there for me over the years. Thank you to my parents, and younger brother and sister, Alex and Elena.

Barbara Dee, for guiding me through the publication process so gracefully and going above and beyond, bringing not only experience but passion behind helping me each step of the way in publishing this book and continuing to build my brand through publications.

Joel Eschenbach, always a friend and mentor as well, thank you for believing in me. I couldn't have done this without your input and everything you did from the graphic design to the cover design and more. -Julie Jelinek, thank you for your encouragement with writing my book, insight, and guidance. Darnell Henderson, a friend and mentor who routinely checks on me and offers insight and motivation.

A special thank you to Sal Ventimaglia, an entrepreneur to whom I owe much guidance. You gave me much confidence as you were able to relate to many of my struggles as an entrepreneur and recognized the potential within each one of my ideas.

Thank you Grant Atkinson, for always helping with each legal step, and looking out for me when I needed it most, being patient even when I couldn't afford legal steps.

Lastly, to my closest friends -I am grateful for each one of you and look forward to many more experiences and memories together.

Life is all about experiences and discovering more about yourself along with the world around you. In my experience I've found that roadtrips, either solo or with loved ones, are crucial for all of these important components. This book will empower you to have experiences to discover much more about yourself and what this beautiful world has to offer, expanding your mind and changing your paradigm while strengthening your relationships. This is the first book of many, along with an associated brand that will empower you and allow you everything you need to simply LIVE. I am grateful for you as a reader and I wish you some epic, future adventures ahead!

Stay updated and interact with me at HowToRoadTripAmerica.com

> *"Adventure is worthwhile in itself."*
>
> —*Aesop*

About the Author

Jonathan Simos is a lifestyle entrepreneur, born in Sarasota, Florida, from a family of Greek origin. He is currently building a personal brand to allow him to share the journey along with each lesson learned as he launches consecutive business ventures. Check out JonSimos.com to follow his journey and stay updated on the development of each venture.

With a passion for traveling and better serving others, Jonathan recognized the necessity for modern road trip resources. Understanding the vast benefits that road trips can provide, and that most individuals don't know where to begin in planning, Jonathan wanted to show that creating life changing road trips and enjoying the wonders that each one brings can be a simple process. He was compelled to create the *How To Road Trip America* series, to ensure each and every road trip adventure is an epic one that creates the memories of a lifetime for you and your loved ones.

This book is the first of a series so don't forget to subscribe to the blog at howtoroadtripamerica.com for additional resources and updates! Make sure to follow the @HowToRoadTripAmerica on instagram and facebook so you don't miss the launching of each book!

> "Choose your dream adventure and live an epic life."
>
> —*Simos #TheRoadTripExpert*

The majestic sunsets of White Sands National Monument In Arizona

CPSIA information can be obtained
at www.ICGtesting.com
Printed in the USA
LVHW072012221220
674730LV00022B/1125